This book belongs to:

_____

Happy Holidays!

BENI'S
TINY TALES

Around the Year in Jewish Holidays

Story and Pictures By
Jane Breskin Zalben

Christy Ottaviano Books
Little, Brown and Company
New York Boston

Roberta Harris, baker extraordinaire and special education teacher,
tested all the recipes in this book for accuracy.

ABOUT THIS BOOK

The illustrations for this book were done in colored pencils, ink, acrylic paints, and watercolors using a triple zero brush on opaline parchment. This book was edited by Christy Ottaviano and designed by Angelie Yap. The production was supervised by Virginia Lawther, and the production editor was Annie McDonnell. The text was set in Sabon LT Std, and the display type is Bulmer MT Std.

Christy Ottaviano Books
Hachette Book Group
1290 Avenue of the Americas, New York, NY 10104
Visit us at LBYR.com

First Edition: August 2023

Christy Ottaviano Books is an imprint of Little, Brown and Company.
The Christy Ottaviano Books name and logo are trademarks of Hachette Book Group, Inc.
The publisher is not responsible for websites (or their content) that are not owned by the publisher.

Little, Brown and Company books may be purchased in bulk for business, educational, or promotional use. For information, please contact your local bookseller or the Hachette Book Group Special Markets Department at special.markets@hbgusa.com.

Library of Congress Cataloging-in-Publication Data
Names: Zalben, Jane Breskin, author, illustrator.
Title: Beni's tiny tales : around the year in Jewish holidays / story and pictures by Jane Breskin Zalben.
Description: First edition. | New York : Little, Brown and Company, 2023. | "A Christy Ottaviano Book." | Audience: Ages 4–8. | Summary: From Rosh Hashanah through Shavuot, Beni and his family celebrate Jewish holidays through the year. Includes craft activities and recipes.
Identifiers: LCCN 2022039637 | ISBN 9780316331777 (hardcover)
Subjects: CYAC: Jews—United States—Fiction. | Holidays—Fiction. | Bears—Fiction. | LCGFT: Short stories.
Classification: LCC PZ7.Z254 Bp 2023 | DDC [E]—dc23
LC record available at https://lccn.loc.gov/2022039637

ISBN: 978-0-316-33177-7

PRINTED IN CHINA

APS

10 9 8 7 6 5 4 3 2 1

To Alexander and Jonathan,
my sweet sons, now grown into wonderful talented men,
and their wives, Marni and Kate, who brought their children—
Penny and Milo, and Liam,
all of whom I am passionate about—
into the world.
And especially, Steven,
to where it all began so long ago.
Words aren't enough.

Author's Note

In March of 2020, when the pandemic started to shut everything down, I began to miss friends and family. At one of our meals—because that was a highlight of our day, and I love to garden, grow vegetables, and cook—my husband, Steve, asked, "What ever happened to Beni's family? What became of all the bears from the series?" It was now decades later. They had grown up. Some had children. Some didn't. Some were married. Some weren't. Their lives were complex, like ours. I emailed my editor, Christy Ottaviano, who knew Beni well. She was the editor on my last published Beni book, twenty-five years ago. Her enthusiasm allowed me to rediscover the family. She suggested, "Have them reflect the world today, having varied experiences and emotions within their extended family."

I have to admit that I love being with people, but I also love being alone. So it was a joy to go into the room where I write and draw and have words pouring forth on the page for this massive undertaking. The work gave me purpose. After I had written ten stories—each one for a Jewish holiday—Christy encouraged me to continue, and said, "Paint the new characters." So I did, with names and personalities. I feel truly fortunate that this is how I got through the pandemic— returning to the fictional family I cherish, creating a modern generation in the world of Beni, a bear with a lot of heart, telling tales of what we all need: love, comfort, humor, empathy, and a foundation of inner strength during hard times. I wrote to Christy, with heartfelt thanks, after completing ten tiny tales. Beni—he's b-a-a-c-k! And so is the whole family, with new members to be discovered. I hope you enjoy reading about them as much as I have loved creating them.

Contents

* All recipes and crafts should be made with adult supervision.

HOLIDAY CALENDAR AROUND THE YEAR

SEPTEMBER	OCTOBER	NOVEMBER	DECEMBER
Rosh Hashanah *Yom Kippur*	*Sukkot* *Shemini Atzeret* *Simchat Torah*		*Chanukah*
JANUARY	FEBRUARY	MARCH	APRIL
	Tu B'Shevat	*Purim*	*Passover*
MAY	JUNE	JULY	AUGUST
Lag B'Omer	*Shavuot*		

Note: Months and years of the Jewish calendar follow the lunar calendar's cycles of the moon and sun. Holidays vary year to year, occurring earlier or later during the months of the more commonly used Gregorian calendar. (For example, Chanukah can fall in late November, but it's usually in December.) I have indicated what month they mostly occur. Holidays begin at sundown the night before. There are other holidays: *Yom Ha'Shoah, Yom Ha'Atzma'ut, Tisha B'Av*. (See glossary.) Included are the most popular holidays celebrated for children.

Beni's Family Tree

MATERNAL

Great-great-grandma Bubbe Zissele
+ Great-great-grandpa Zaide

Great-aunt Rivka
+ Great-uncle Solly

Aunt Masha

Aunt Brancha

Great-grandma Mindel
+ Great-grandpa Fishel

Tante Rose
+ Uncle Schmuel

Mama (Yael)
+ Papa (Schmulka)

Cousin Max
+ Avi

Cousin Rosie

Beni
+ Emma

Sara
+ Harry

no kids (yet)

no kids

Penny

Milo

Liam

PATERNAL

Great-great-grandma Sadie
+ Great-great-grandpa Chaim

Nana
+ Great-grandpa Gus

Uncle Leo
+ Aunt Chana

Aunt Gloria

Aunt Gertie
+ Uncle Hymie
Moishe (Hymie's brother)

Great-aunt Carrie
+ Great-uncle Harry

Cousin Goldie
+ Abe

Cousin Molly
(divorced)

Cousin Sam
+ Luna

Noa

Sophie

Baby Becky
(+ one on the way)

* Uncle Gus and Aunt Izzy are such dear old friends, they're like family to us.

Family Portrait Photo Credit © Bearinski Studio of Brooklyn.

(Bottom row left to right) Milo, Penny, Liam, Noa, Sophie, Baby Becky
(Second row left to right) Great-grandma Mindel, Mama, Papa, Luna, Sam, Molly
(Third row left to right) Rosie, Beni, Emma, Goldie, Sara
(Top row left to right) Avi, Max, Abe, Harry

INTRODUCTION

The air was cold and crisp, and smelled of winter:
pine needles, cinnamon sticks, and baked apples.
Tonight was the first night of Chanukah.
Beni and Emma's children were getting ready.
Penny raced around the house. "Is it sundown yet?"
Milo wondered, "Can I choose colors for the candles?"
And cousin Liam, who was sleeping over,
asked, "What time are my parents coming?"
When the whole family arrived—aunts, uncles, cousins,
grandparents, and even a great-great-grandparent—
there was so much hugging and kissing,
the family nearly missed the start of the holiday!
They lit the menorah, said prayers, sang songs,
and spun the dreidel as Beni and his sister, Sara,
made different kinds of *latkes* from their childhood.
"Are there presents for all of us?" whispered Penny.
"Yes," said Beni as Milo, the youngest, handed them out.
They would get a small gift for each of the eight nights.

Tonight, each child got a big calendar made of thick,
shiny paper showing Jewish holidays around the year.
"The new year begins in September? Not now?" asked
cousin Liam.
Beni nodded. "Let's see what the holidays are, my little cubs.
And we'll make up a tiny tale for each one!" he added.
Beni flipped to the first page and began.

ROSH HASHANAH

The holiday of Rosh Hashanah means "Head of the Year." It is the beginning of the Jewish New Year, usually in September. Also called "The Birthday of the World," this holiday marks the start of the ten Days of Awe, which end with Yom Kippur. Rosh Hashanah and Yom Kippur are referred to as the High Holy Days. The *shofar*, a ram's horn, is blown many times during the synagogue service to announce the new year. Its sound is supposed to awaken the congregation to pay attention and become their better selves. Jews celebrate by sharing festive meals with family and friends, and greeting each other with the saying: "*L'shanah tovah*. Happy New Year! To a sweet, good year!" The community gathers to participate in *tashlikh*, an outdoor ceremony in which people toss bits of bread into a moving body of water like a brook or river, symbolizing the casting away of bad deeds to begin the year with a fresh clean slate—starting over.

Old photo by Papa

BeniBearBakes.com

Beni looked through his recipes. "Baking's my thing."

"Remember the time you made latkes?" said Penny.

"And one landed on your sister Sara's head?" she reminded him.

"Didn't you go around calling her Mrs. Potato Head for a month?"

"And when you flipped pizza dough in the air and it stuck on our ceiling," Milo said. "And then the dough fell on Baby Becky, and everyone said she looked like Baby Burrito instead."

"Moving right along . . ." Beni rolled his eyes. "I'm making a *challah* for the new year," he said. "Maybe some *mandelbrot*, *rugelach*, and sponge or honey cake. We'll see how the day goes."

"Knock yourself out." Emma winked. "I'm going to work."

So Penny and Milo decided to help their father.

Beni lined up all the ingredients, while Penny and Milo showed off their baking skills: beating, stirring, kneading.

Sticky dough settled on Milo's nose. He flicked it at Penny.
So she tossed a raisin in his direction. On purpose this time,
he pitched a pinch of dough at her, squealing, "Food fight!"
Adjusting their aprons and torn chef's hats, the children threw
ingredients until flour dusted them and most of the kitchen.
Beni hollered, "Claws and paws in the air!
What's the holiday of Rosh Hashanah about, again?"

Penny glanced down. "Beginning the new year with a fresh start."
"Learning from our mistakes. Being kind to each other," said Milo.
"Exactly," replied Beni. "I'm sorry I yelled at you both."
"I'm sorry." Milo turned toward Penny.
"I'm sorry too." Penny turned toward Milo.
"We're sorry, Daddy," they repeated together.
And they all gave each other a messy sandwich hug.

Later, when their mother came home from work, everything looked spotless. "How are my sweet little chefs doing?" she asked.

"Fine," they both said, looking up at her innocently.

"And how's my big chef doing? Did you have a nice day?" Emma asked Beni, who looked as if he was ready to *plotz*.

"Let's put it this way," Beni yawned, "history repeated itself."

"Like you and your sister, Sara, behaved?" Emma asked.

"Who, me?" Now it was Beni's turn to look at her innocently.

"Something smells delicious." Emma noticed the golden round raisin challah tucked in a large straw basket.

"I could make you a website for all your recipes.

How about BeniBearBakes.com?" She gave Beni a big kiss.

"That would be a nice way to start off the year." Beni kissed her back
and wiped a smudge of dough off Milo's forehead.

Then he plopped on the couch and began to snore.

His family covered him with a cozy plaid blanket.

Beni dreamt of dipping the challah into honey, hoping the coming year
was sweet and good and full of joy for everyone in his family circle,
and for everyone outside it, too.

HAPPY NEW YEAR GREETING CARDS

Send greeting cards to each other through snail mail or over the internet before the holiday, wishing friends and family a Happy New Year! Here are some ideas for making your own card.

1. Take a piece of paper, any size, and fold in half. (It can be construction paper or plain white paper.)
   Optional: You can add pages to your card by folding one or more additional pieces of paper, tucking them inside the main/exterior piece, and sewing down the fold in the center with red wool or embroidery thread or ribbon. Knot and cut at each end.

2. Draw an apple or make a collage of apples that you cut out and paste. Or paint a piece of Bubble Wrap mustard gold to resemble a beehive. Cut and glue to the front of your card. Make a little bumblebee no bigger than 2 inches long by ¾ inch wide. Draw or build using black and yellow fuzzy pipe cleaners. For each color, cut three ¾-inch strips. Place alternating colors next to each other to form the bee's stripes. Use clear glue to hold together.

3. Write (or have an adult or older sibling help write) something nice inside your greeting card—a wish you might have for the new year.

HONEY CAKE MUFFINS

Beni's friend Kate has a rooftop beehive. Bees make honey and pollinate flowers. Kate gave Beni a jar as a shalach manot *gift during Purim. He saved the honey to use in his baking for the new year! And then he also used the backyard maple syrup he had made during Tu B'Shevat.*

3 cups unbleached all-purpose flour, sifted

1 teaspoon baking soda

1 teaspoon baking powder

3 large eggs, separated

1 cup granulated sugar

¼ cup vegetable oil

Juice of one lemon

1 cup honey

1 cup coffee, brewed

1 teaspoon maple syrup

1 teaspoon ground ginger

1 teaspoon cinnamon

½ teaspoon ground allspice

½ teaspoon orange zest

1 teaspoon cream of tartar

1 tablespoon ground almonds

1. Preheat oven to 350 degrees Fahrenheit.
2. In a large bowl, sift flour, baking soda, and baking powder together.
3. In another large bowl, beat egg yolks and sugar 2 minutes until lemon color. Add oil, lemon juice, honey, coffee, and maple syrup. Stir.
4. Add spices to honey mixture. Combine both bowls together.
5. In a separate bowl, beat egg whites with cream of tartar until stiff peaks form. Fold egg whites into batter with spatula, gently adding ground almonds.
6. Line muffin tin with paper liners. Pour into each muffin or cupcake cup until two thirds full (or use an ice cream scoop), leaving room for muffin to rise, almost doubling in height.
7. Bake 25 minutes on a rack in the middle of the oven or until muffins are a light golden brown.

Yield: about 2 dozen muffins

Beni's Round Raisin-Apple Challah

A round raisin challah symbolizes the cycle of life. This bread is more special than the braided Friday-night challah we normally eat on Shabbat because it is dipped in honey so the new year will be a sweet one. Alongside the challah, apples are also dipped in honey to be sweet for the coming year. Beni got the idea to place apples on top of the challah from his neighbor Marni, who is quite the baker!

2 packages of dry yeast dissolved in 2 cups of warm water

Pinch of sugar

3 large eggs

1 egg white (reserve yolk)

1 teaspoon salt (optional portion)

2 tablespoons vegetable oil

⅔ cup honey

9 cups unbleached flour

1 cup dark raisins

½ teaspoon cinnamon

1 sweet red apple, peeled, cored, thinly sliced (optional)

1. Dissolve yeast in 2 cups warm (not boiling) water or use a food thermometer to around 105 degrees Fahrenheit. Add sugar. Stir. Set aside at room temperature for 10 minutes until the liquid foams.
2. Beat 3 eggs and 1 egg white. (Reserve yolk for later.) Add salt, oil, and honey to mixture and continue beating.
3. Put flour in large bowl. Indent center, making a well with your fist. Gradually add yeast mixture to flour, stirring center with a wooden spoon until it is fully absorbed. Stir in liquid from Step 2.
4. Mix by hand. Fold in raisins and cinnamon. (Sprinkle lightly with flour if dough is sticky.) When dough is smooth, place in a greased bowl. Cover with a dish towel. Keep in warm spot for 1–2 hours. Let dough rise until it doubles in size. Punch dough down.

5. Knead dough for 5 minutes on a floured board or surface until the dough tightens and is no longer sticky. Divide into 2 balls. Form each ball into a roll between your fingers to make a snakelike rope about 18 inches long. Shape circle by twisting the rope into a spiral with the end of the snake tucked under the round.

6. Let dough rise again, uncovered, for 1 hour on greased baking pan or cookie sheet until doubled in size.

7. Preheat oven to 375 degrees Fahrenheit.

8. Egg wash: Gently beat the reserved egg yolk with 1 teaspoon cold water. Coat the loaves with the egg mixture using a clean, 1-inch pastry brush. This will give the challah a golden glaze when it is baked.

9. Cut circle halves of an apple into paper-thin slices with a knife or mandolin to decorate the top of challah, partially layering slice over slice.

10. Bake for 25 minutes or until golden brown.

Yield: 2 loaves

Emma's Rugelach

Emma makes the best rugelach. So Beni is giving credit where credit is due. The family makes the rugelach together, then sometimes freezes it before the holiday because they are shvach—tired—from so much cooking. Rugelach seem hard to make. But guess what? It's easy and fun. One year, Cousin Rosie was coming over; she's allergic to nuts. Since then, Emma makes sure she knows who's visiting before she adds walnuts. On the holiday, Beni heats the rugelach in the oven, and they disappear faster than you can say, "L'shanah tovah!"

Dough

2 sticks unsalted butter, softened to room temperature

1 8-ounce package of cream cheese, softened to room temperature

½ teaspoon vanilla extract

The peel of 1 fresh orange, finely grated

½ teaspoon salt (optional; Papa is on a salt-free diet!)

2 cups unbleached all-purpose flour, sifted

Filling

⅔ cup walnuts, finely chopped (optional)

½ cup granulated sugar

½ cup raisins or currants

2 teaspoons cinnamon

Other Ingredients

⅓ cup raspberry jam or apricot preserves

1 bag mini chocolate chips

Dried cranberries

1. With a mixer, cream together butter and cream cheese, adding vanilla and orange zest.
2. Add salt to the flour. Sift.
3. Gradually add flour to creamed mixture. Blend all ingredients.
4. After sticky dough is formed, knead on floured surface into a ball. Wrap dough in waxed paper. Refrigerate for about 2 hours to harden.
5. Preheat oven to 350 degrees Fahrenheit.

6. Remove the dough from refrigerator. Divide into 3 parts. With a rolling pin, roll out one section of dough on a floured surface until about ⅛-inch thick. Place a large pie pan or plate upside down on top of the dough and cut around outer edge with a knife to form a large circle like a pizza pie. (Set aside extra dough to patch any holes.) Repeat the process for the other two parts of dough.

7. In a small bowl, mix together the filling ingredients. Set aside.

8. With a spatula (or the back of a large spoon), spread jam of choice on each circular dough to lightly coat its flattened surface.

9. Sprinkle ⅓ of the filling mixture of walnuts, sugar, and cinnamon across each flat dough circle. And then add mini chocolate chips, or dried cranberries, or raisins or currants—or all of them!—on top.

10. With a pizza cutter or sharp knife, cut each circle into 12 triangles. Roll each triangle into a crescent shape starting with the wide end.

11. Dip each crescent-shaped rugelach into the sugar/cinnamon mixture.

12. Place on greased or parchment-lined cookie sheets.

13. Bake for 20 minutes or until rugelach is a light tan and the bottom of the pastry is still soft.

Yield: 3 dozen, depending on size

Special Note: Emma makes the dough ahead of time, freezes it, and then thaws it when she and Beni are ready to bake. She uses the same dough for pies and quiches when they have a light dairy meal, which is perfect for the "break fast" meal of Yom Kippur.

Pareve: You can use a cream cheese substitute if you are having a meat meal, or swap out butter with kosher margarine.

YOM KIPPUR

The ten days of the High Holy Days end with Yom Kippur, the Day of Atonement, the most solemn day of the Jewish New Year and one of the most culturally significant. It is a time to think of what we have done in the past year, how to make up for a wrongdoing, and how we can become better in the coming year. Forgiveness. The holiday begins at sundown and ends the next day at sundown. On *erev* Yom Kippur—the night before the holiday—a traditional meal is served before sundown. Prayers begin on the eve of this night with *Kol Nidre* service in the synagogue. People pray and fast until the sun sets the next night. (Adults don't eat or drink anything during this time. Children and older or infirmed people are not required to fast.) Most Jews attend synagogue all day. At the end of the holiday on Yom Kippur evening, a light meal of dairy, vegetables, *kugel* puddings, and bagels—called a "Break Fast"—is enjoyed by family and friends to end the fast.

GOOD DEED COUPONS

Penny announced, "This year, I'm going to fast."

"Not in a million years," said Milo.

"I bet I could hold off on sweets for the whole day."

Milo looked at Penny like she was from another planet.

"This, I have to see," he smirked and gave a chuckle.

"I could at least try." Penny walked off in a huff.

Beni overheard them. "When I was little, I made coupons
to give to each family member: Papa, Mama, and Sara.
I wrote a good deed I could do on each one."

"Like what?" asked Milo.

"Papa's coupon said: *Good for taking the trash out for a week.* But he suggested I practice the piano every day instead."

"Did you like that idea better?" asked Milo. Beni smiled.

"We did a duet: Papa on the ukulele. Me on the piano. Mama wore her best dress on opening night. I gave her a coupon, too: *Good for one private concert in the living room.* Obviously, we performed to tremendous applause."

"What about Aunt Sara?" Milo snuggled up to his father.

"Sara's coupon said: *Good for not bothering my little sister. Ever.*"

Emma peeked in. "And how did that work out for you?"

"No comment." Beni furrowed his eyebrows, mouthing, *Thanks.*

"I guess," he suggested, "I could make a new coupon for my sister."

Coupon for Sara
Sorry I called you Mrs. Potato Head
(and a million other things)
Good for one tray of delicious potato kugel
or potato nik minus the schmaltz (chicken fat!)
Redeemable now.

"What does that mean?" Milo looked over at his father.

"She can ask for my gift by turning in her coupon."

"And how many years later is this?" asked Emma.

Beni lowered his voice to almost a whisper. "Over thirty?"

"I think she's owed a hundred kugels by now!" Emma teased him.

"I have too many bad things to list," admitted Penny, adding,

"I shouldn't have tossed raisins at you, Milo. I will act nicer.

Coupon for Milo: *Good for one lanyard rope that I wove in camp.*"

Beni's eyes filled with tears, remembering it took her all summer to make.

Milo grinned. "Thanks, Penny! I shouldn't have thrown dough at you.

Here's a coupon from me: *Good for no fights. One whole year.*"

"Only one year?" repeated Penny. "Seriously?"

"I have to see how I feel next year," said Milo.

"In the next hour is more like it," Penny shot back.

"S-o-r-r-y I said that!" she added.

Beni and Emma bit their lower lips, trying not to laugh.

As time went by, Penny realized she had skipped a meal.

"I think I'm going to faint," she said to her parents.

"Do I have to think up another coupon for not fasting all day?"

"I have a family coupon: *Good for one group hug,*" Beni said.

How to Make a Good Deed Coupon Booklet

The children made their coupon booklets before the holiday because Yom Kippur should be a quiet day of thought and rest.

1. Take 4 pieces of plain white paper. Fold in half to make an 8-page booklet. (Two sides for each piece of paper.)
2. Staple or sew down the center fold with an embroidery needle using thick colored button thread or wool. Knot ends.
3. Put the name of the person to whom the gift is for on the front page.
4. On the next left-hand page write: *I'm sorry for…*
5. On the facing page write a Good Deed you want to do for that person to make up for any wrongdoings. Draw art of the act you'd like to do and add borders around the page.
6. Wrap in tissue paper and tie with a ribbon. Then give!

Beni and Emma's Hits for the Holiday

Beni said to Emma, "We have to decide what we're serving for the Break Fast meal. Sara and Harry are making noodle kugel. I'm doing a potato kugel for Sara." Beni looked contrite. "Goldie's bringing her usual—chocolate *babka*; Molly, *kasha varnishkas*; and Sam, bagels and *bialys* and cream cheese." "Ask for the walnut-and-raisin spread," Emma reminded him. Beni continued, "Max and Avi bought assorted cheeses. Rosie's doing her *babaganoush*, *hummus*, and *falafel* balls with homemade pitas. And Uncle Gus is supplying lox, carp, and whitefish from his deli downtown: Gus & Daughters. Emma's good friend Izzy's baking a salmon." "There's leftover challah from Rosh Hashanah, so I'm making French toast." Emma piped in, "I saved some rugelach dough in the freezer, so I'll make different kinds of quiches. And this year, we're giving your parents and Great-grandma Mindel a real cooking break!" Emma insisted. Beni sliced some of his leftover challah while Emma defrosted her dough.

POTATO KUGEL FOR SARA

4–5 large Idaho or russet potatoes

3 extra-large eggs, beaten

2–3 tablespoons vegetable oil

⅓ cup matzoh meal

½ teaspoon salt (optional)

½ teaspoon ground pepper

½ medium onion, minced

2 cloves garlic, mashed

1. Preheat oven to 375 degrees Fahrenheit.
2. Peel potatoes. Shred them in a food processor or by hand.
3. In a separate bowl, beat eggs, adding oil, and matzoh meal.
4. Measure in pepper and salt. Add finely chopped onion.
5. Peel garlic cloves. Mash with back of spoon and add to mixture.
6. Stir in potatoes. Combine mixtures. Pour into a greased baking dish, approximately 8 x 12 inches. Bake for 1 hour until golden brown.

Yield: Serves 12 (Cut into squares after it has rested for about 5 minutes.)

FANCY-SCHMANCY FRENCH TOAST

1 large challah, sliced

3–4 large eggs, beaten

2 tablespoons milk

½ teaspoon vanilla extract

1 teaspoon ground cinnamon

Unsalted butter, softened for greasing

Confectioner's sugar (optional)

Preserves or jam or maple syrup
  (for dipping French toast)

Sprig of mint to decorate (optional)

1 strawberry, thinly sliced (optional)

1. Slice one challah according to how thick you like the pieces.
   (Beni's family likes them in wedges about ½-inch or more thick.)
2. Beat eggs, milk, vanilla extract, and cinnamon in a large bowl.
3. Soak challah in the liquid mixture until bread is soft.
4. Grease a large frying pan with butter. Fry each slice of bread on both sides.
   Remove when lightly brown and serve on a plate.
5. Dust confectioner's sugar on top of each slice (optional).
   Or dip pieces into raspberry jam or maple syrup!

Yield: Depends on how large your challah is, and how thick you slice it.
Double the recipe for a crowd!

*For fancy-schmancy French toast, add a thinly sliced strawberry and a mint
leaf on the side.*

HOMEMADE QUICHE

Emma rolled out the leftover rugelach dough for the quiche crust.

Vegetable or olive oil for frying
½ cup spinach (or zucchini, or
  broccoli, and/or beet greens),
  cooked and drained
2 large garlic cloves, peeled and
  minced (optional)
½ cup sliced mushrooms (washed
  and dried, for sautéing)
3–4 eggs (depending on size), beaten
1 cup milk

1 teaspoon ground nutmeg
Dash of pepper and salt (optional)
8 grape tomatoes cut in half
1 6-ounce jar of artichoke hearts,
  drained
Sprinkle tarragon or oregano or
  rosemary or chopped chives
Shredded cheese of your choice to
  garnish top of quiche

1. Preheat oven to 350 degrees Fahrenheit.
2. *Crust*: Use rugelach dough recipe. Roll out to ⅛-inch thick. Press dinner
   plate on dough. Cut around edge. Place onto buttered 9-inch round quiche,
   tart, or pie pan. Pinch dough perimeter with thumb and forefinger to make
   scalloped edge. Bake in oven for 7 minutes. (You can weigh down dough
   with dried beans at bottom of crust to prevent rising while cooking, and
   then discard beans.) Remove. Set aside.
3. *Filling*: Coat large frying pan with oil. Sauté garlic until tender. Stir in
   vegetables over medium heat for about 3 minutes, adding sliced mushrooms.
4. Spread mixture at bottom of crust in quiche, tart, or pie pan.
5. In a mixing bowl, beat eggs, milk, and nutmeg, with a dash of salt and pepper.
6. Pour in pan. Spread tomatoes and artichokes on top. Sprinkle spices.
7. Bake for 1 hour. Ten minutes before end of baking time, sprinkle shredded
   cheese on top of quiche and continue to bake.
8. Let it rest for 5 minutes. Cut into wedges. Serve with tossed salad.

Yield: 1 large quiche (about 8 servings)

*Note: Beni adds peppers—hot and sweet—to his quiche with sliced jalapeño
cheese to make it spicy.*

EMMA'S SALAD AND POMEGRANATE DRESSING

The pomegranate originated in Iran, extending all the way to northern India and the Mediterranean area. The fruit has been a symbol in Judaism since ancient times. (It also has significance in Christianity, Islam, Buddhism, and other ancient religions.) Its seeds are a symbol of life. Traditionally, they are eaten during the Jewish New Year of Rosh Hashanah because they have approximately 613 seeds, and there are 613 commandments (mitzvot) in the Torah. Emma displays pomegranates throughout the High Holy Days in a bowl on the dining-room table.

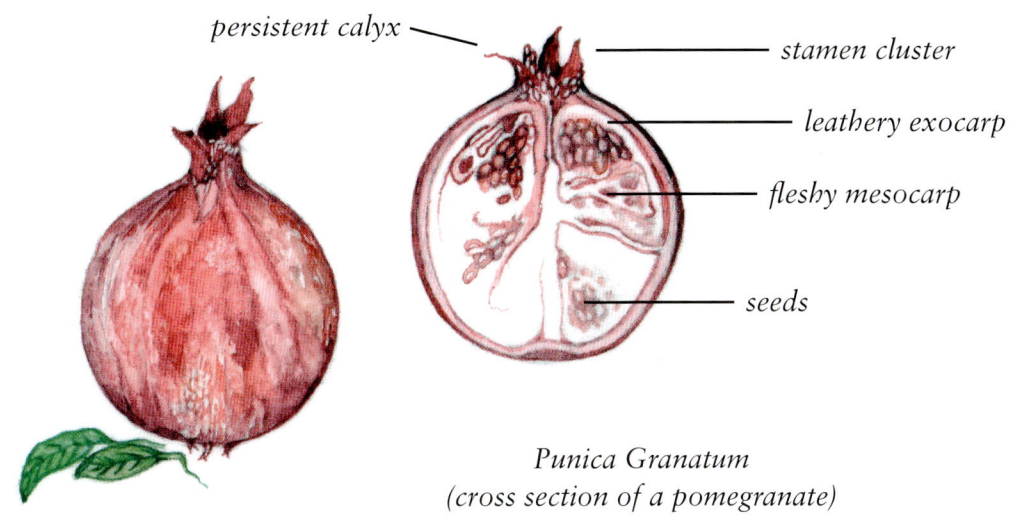

persistent calyx

stamen cluster

leathery exocarp

fleshy mesocarp

seeds

Punica Granatum
(cross section of a pomegranate)

Salad: Emma likes to add pomegranate seeds to tossed lettuce along with sliced strawberries, raspberries, or blackberries. Beni adds olives, endive, chopped radicchio, avocado, cucumbers, beets, and goat cheese.

Salad dressing: Mix ½ cup pomegranate juice (or ½ teaspoon pomegranate molasses), ¼ cup apple cider vinegar, ¼ cup olive oil, 1–2 tablespoons lemon juice (to taste), and ¼ teaspoon Dijon mustard (to taste).

Optional: Add ¼ teaspoon tarragon or dried oregano, a dash of pepper or salt. (Emma loves pomegranates so much—"like little red-ruby-colored jewels"—she puts the juice on chicken, in a rib rub marinade, and in baked goods.)

Sukkot and Shemini Atzeret

Sukkot starts five days after Yom Kippur. This Festival of Booths or Tabernacles is a harvest festival lasting seven days, usually occurring in October. A *sukkah* (or temporary hut) is built. A family eats, drinks, and sometimes sleeps in it, as a reminder of how the Israelites lived in the wilderness wandering the desert. The sukkah can have three or four sides with walls of bamboo poles or canvas, and a loose roof of tree branches, evergreens, or palms. Branches should cover the hut during the day to make shade but be open enough to see the stars at night.

Following the seven joyous days of Sukkot is Shemini Atzeret. *Shemini* means "eighth day." It is referred to as "the Eighth Day of Assembly." Many consider it the end of Sukkot. There is a special prayer for rain.

Before the Pilgrims came to the Americas in 1620, they read about this ancient harvest festival in the Bible and modeled their first American Thanksgiving on the holiday of Sukkot.

SOPHIE'S SUKKAH SLEEPOVER

Cousin Molly said to Sophie, "Would you like to ask all your cousins to decorate, eat, and then sleep in our sukkah tonight?"

Sophie's eyes widened. "*A campout?* Yes!"

That afternoon they arrived with their sleeping bags.

They strung cranberries and popcorn and made paper chains.

They placed candles inside scooped pumpkins that they left on the walkway to the hut where they'd have their sleepover.

Molly added rice-paper lanterns that would light up at night.

She hung everything from the ceiling covered with pine boughs.

The children breathed in the sweet fragrance of apples and lemons when they went inside the hut to eat. *It's a smell they'll remember*, thought Molly, *even when they're old*.

After dinner, everybody helped clean up and get ready for bed.
Liam wanted to sleep next to Penny, and so did Milo.
So Penny put her sleeping bag on the ground between them.
But Sophie wanted to be near her, too, to tell secrets.
That was a problem for Noa. "I also want to be near Penny!"
And Baby Becky, who was too young to stay overnight with them,
crawled in for a few minutes. They worked it out when
Penny realized they could sleep in a circle, toes touching.
They peeked at the stars and the harvest moon above,
which looked like a large lemon slice hanging in the sky.

"Can you imagine what it must have been like to sleep for forty years in a desert like the Jews did in olden times?" asked Milo as a sudden gust of wind swept across the backyard.

The sukkah shook. Beads rattled. Lanterns flickered.

Moments later, droplets of rain poked through the roof.

"I'm scared," Milo whispered. "I have to go to the bathroom."

And then it began to pour. Hard. Like a monsoon!

Cousin Molly ran outside to get everyone safely indoors.
She made them warm apple cider with cinnamon sticks, while they
munched on Sophie's apple-cranberry-orange-lemon loaf.
In the nice warm house, they told ghost stories inside a tent made of
blankets instead of tree branches and palms.

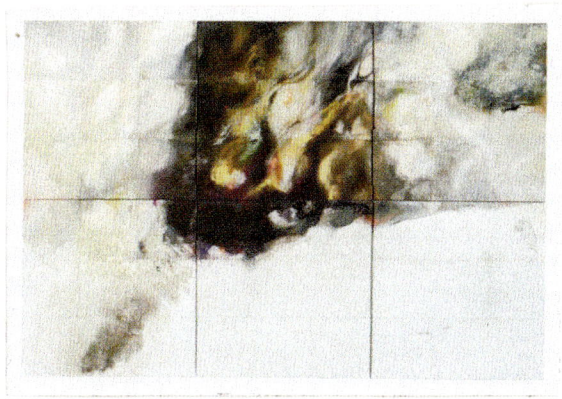

HOW TO DECORATE A SUKKAH

There are four festival symbols, called the Four Species: palm, willow, myrtle, and etrog (or citron). The etrog *symbolizes those who study the Torah and do good deeds. The shaking of the* lulav *(palm branch) in different directions symbolizes that God is everywhere. Many decorate the top of their sukkahs with palms.*

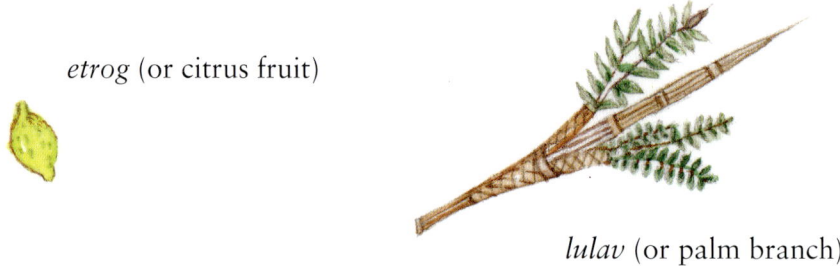

etrog (or citrus fruit)

lulav (or palm branch)

SEVEN MAJOR FRUITS OF ISRAEL

wheat, barley, grapes, olives, dates, figs, and pomegranates

OBJECTS FOR THE SUKKAH

(You can hang fruits and vegetables, and make place mats for meals inside your sukkah.)

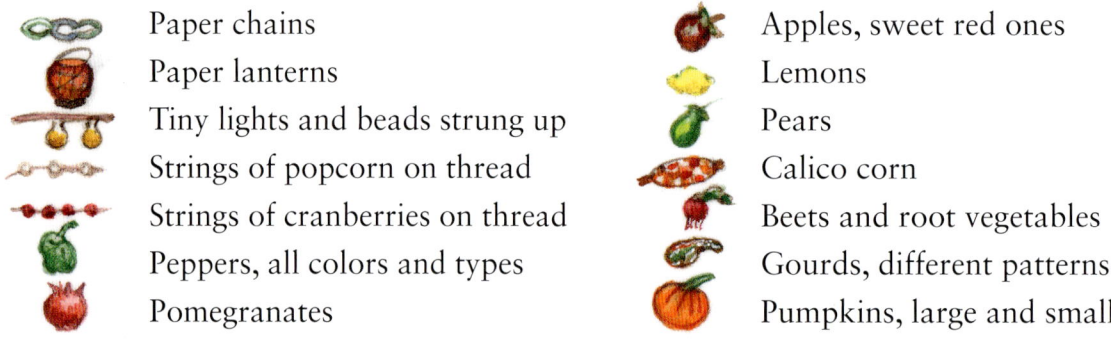

Paper chains

Paper lanterns

Tiny lights and beads strung up

Strings of popcorn on thread

Strings of cranberries on thread

Peppers, all colors and types

Pomegranates

Apples, sweet red ones

Lemons

Pears

Calico corn

Beets and root vegetables

Gourds, different patterns

Pumpkins, large and small

Apple-Cranberry-Orange-Lemon Loaf

Sophie chose this recipe to bake with her mother, Molly, before the cousins came to decorate. They added lemon to represent the etrog (citron—citrus fruit), one of the Four Species. The aroma in the kitchen after they finished baking was almost as wonderful as the smell inside their sukkah.

---

1 large red apple, peeled and diced

1 cup fresh cranberries

¾ cup chopped walnuts (optional)

1 lemon, grated rind for zest

1 orange, grated rind for zest

1 extra-large egg, beaten

½ teaspoon vanilla or almond extract

2 tablespoons butter, melted

¾ cup orange juice

1 cup granulated sugar

2 cups unbleached all-purpose flour, sifted

1 teaspoon baking powder

½ teaspoon baking soda

½ teaspoon ground cinnamon

(Note: Add a few lemon peels, apple slices, or cranberries to decorate the top of the loaf. One year, Molly substituted orange zest for the lemon. It was sweeter! This year, she used both the lemon and orange zest together. Yummy.)

1. Preheat oven to 350 degrees Fahrenheit.
2. Combine apples, cranberries, walnuts, lemon zest, and orange zest in a bowl. (This time, Molly added finely chopped nuts.) Set aside.
3. Beat egg until frothy in a mixer, adding vanilla, butter, orange juice, and sugar.
4. Sift together flour, baking powder, and baking soda. Add cinnamon.
5. In mixer, gradually add dry ingredients to wet. Blend until smooth.
6. Gently stir in apple-cranberry-nut-zest mixture.
7. Pour batter into 4½-by-13-inch greased bread pan (or two 5-by-9-inch pans; the loaves will come out lower in height). Bake for 1 hour or until top of loaf splits slightly. (Test with a toothpick or skewer by inserting into the center as deep as possible. Then remove. If the toothpick—or skewer—is dry, the loaf is done!)

Yield: 1 long, large loaf or 2 small loaves

שִׂמְחָה תּוֹרָה

SIMCHAT TORAH

Simchat Torah follows right after Sukkot, usually occurring in mid-October. The reading cycle of the Torah has come to the end and now it starts again from the beginning. *Simchat Torah* means "Joy of the Torah." All the Torah scrolls are taken out of the ark and carried around the synagogue in a parade up and down the aisles, where children wave paper flags. There is singing, dancing, and everyone enjoys eating jelly or candy apples on sticks at the end of the service. Some families give children jelly apples to taste the sweetness of this holiday, which lasts one day—from sundown to the next sundown. For some in Israel and Reform Judaism, the holidays of Shemini Atzerat and Simchat Torah are often combined into a single day after the end of Sukkot.

A TEENY-TINY TALE

Beni said, "This is a teeny-tiny tale."

"Okay," said the cousins, giving him their full attention.

"Simchat Torah is one of my favorite holidays. When I was little, Papa held a Torah in the synagogue, parading it in the aisles as I followed him waving a paper flag, humming along.

When it was time for the jelly apples, a loose baby tooth of mine that had been wiggling for weeks fell out after one bite.

It slid across the temple's dance floor during a wild *horah*!"

"Oh no!" Sophie cried out, touching her first wobbly tooth.

"I couldn't find it to put in my Tooth Fairy Treasure Chest. Since that day, I've never eaten another jelly apple."

"That's not a good story," Penny said, shaking her head.

"Did the tooth fairy still come?" added Noa, looking concerned.

"Yes. She left me a soft caramel-and-chocolate apple instead."

"So it has a happy ending," Liam said with a wide grin.

"It does," said Beni. "Although my sister, Sara, called me 'the Toothless Wonder of Whitestone' for a whole week. I still love this holiday. But I say to all of you, Beware!"— and the cousins leaned in closer—"Bite at your own risk!"

BENI'S CANDY CARAMEL APPLES

Jelly apples are the big item on Simchat Torah. Beni prefers caramel! Sara loves chocolate-dipped apples. Beni made five candy apples for Penny, Milo, Liam, Noa, and Sophie. Baby Becky barely has teeth. So that's a plus; they figured she was a perfect candidate to lick a jelly apple. Some of the cousins drew blue-and-white Israeli flags to wave (attaching a chopstick to the flag drawing) while Beni was cooking on the stovetop.

5 McIntosh apples

1 cup granulated sugar

¾ cup dark corn syrup

1 cup cream

2 tablespoons butter or margarine

1 teaspoon vanilla extract

Thick wooden bamboo skewer
   sticks, 6 inches long

Walnuts, finely chopped
   (optional for decorating)

1. Wash, dry, and remove stems from apples. Pierce the center of each apple with 1 wooden skewer stick.
2. In a pot, cook sugar, syrup, cream, and butter for a few minutes over low flame without stirring. Add vanilla extract.
3. Then stir gently until smooth mixture thickens.
4. Dip apple into mixture and turn it around to coat surface. Remove. Hold apple by skewer and rotate in the air to cool the brown caramel.
5. Roll apple in finely chopped nuts and place on waxed paper to dry.

Yield: 5 caramel apples. Increase ingredients by number of guests, who can dip and make their own versions!

Note: Sara melts dark, milk, or white chocolate instead in a double boiler until smooth, ready for coating. She dips the apple, then swirls it in finely chopped nuts or shredded coconut. One year, she tried both caramel and chocolate! Perfect.

CHANUKAH

Chanukah, called the Festival of Lights, can start from late November or December, and lasts for eight days. A candle is lit on the *menorah* for each of the nights by the *shammash*—a center "helper candle."

The holiday commemorates the Maccabee warriors' victory over the tyrant King Antiochus IV, who wanted the Israelites to worship the many idols of Greek gods instead of praying to their one God. But Judah Maccabee fought back. This triumph returned the Jews to the Temple in Jerusalem, which was ruined after years of war. It was rebuilt and the Eternal Flame was relit. There was enough oil to burn for one day during the Feast of Dedication (Chanukah means "dedication"), but a great miracle happened: the Eternal Flame burned for eight days. During the holiday, Jews are reminded of how Judaism has survived for over two thousand years through many hard times in history. Foods fried in oil, such as potato pancakes (*latkes*) and jelly doughnuts (*sufganiyot*), are eaten as a reminder of this miracle.

All the parents when they were children.

CHANUKAH HUNT

One late winter afternoon a storm began to stir.

The news said: "Stay home. Stay inside. Stay safe!"

Papa, known as the "latke maven" in the family for potato pancakes,

called every single cousin and said, "When your parents were younger

we had a latke contest.

Everyone made different kinds of latkes in a fry-off.

This year, each family could do that in their own home!"

And that is exactly what they did.

Everyone got online to celebrate, but still cooked together.

Papa added a pinch of HOT pepper flakes and a diced tomatillo to his latkes.

Mama made classic plain potato latkes served with homemade applesauce and sour cream on the side.

Cousin Rosie made Indian latkes—*falouris*—with chickpea flour, and used spicy-chunky apple chutney instead of applesauce.

Max fried breaded artichoke hearts alongside Avi's sugary puffs of zeppole, reminding them both of Italy, where they met.

Beni's family loves jelly doughnut holes best! So does Sara's, Goldie's, Molly's, and Sam's. But not Great-grandma Mindel!

Mindel had trouble getting online. She gave directions over the phone for her vegetable latkes and kept them in the oven to stay warm while everyone else fried theirs.

At sundown, they all said the first blessing as each cousin lit the menorah in their own house and put it on a windowsill. Everyone sang holiday songs and ate and ate.

When it was time to play dreidel, there were special guests! Sasha and Christopher—old friends—got on the computer too!

"How many years has it been?" shouted Beni and Sara. "Too many!" they shouted back.

They all learned how to spin a dreidel—but this time Beni's and Sara's kids showed the others how to play.

When it was time for the gifts,
Beni had a brilliant idea.

Beni and Emma walked around with their
computer, holding the screen up in the air behind
Penny and Milo as they searched everywhere.

"Each parent hides a gift for the first night
for each child. Then the kids hunt
for them while the parents follow!"

Milo walked in farther and reached up.
"Cold!" shouted Emma.
So he reached down.
"Hot!" she cried out.

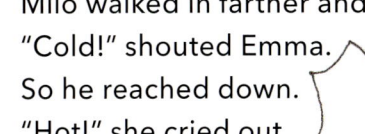

"You're getting warm," said Beni as
Penny and Milo went in the front closet,
moving piles of boxes aside.
"Warmer," he added.

Milo moved snow boots and looked inside.
"Boiling!" Beni and Emma shouted.
"Found it!" screamed Milo, holding his present.
Inside was a bag of chocolate coins wrapped in gold foil.
"Chanukah *gelt*! And a dreidel carved in wood."

It was Penny's turn. She saw another package.
"A diary! To tell my own stories!" Penny smiled wide.
Each family watched the others hunt for their gifts.

Milo began to cry big heartfelt tears.
"What's wrong?" asked Beni and Emma.
"I miss eating together.
Finding our presents together.
Spinning the dreidel together.
Being a whole family together."

"But we are a whole family together!" everyone replied.
"Just in a different way." Papa tried to soothe him.
"Next year, can we be together?
In the same place?" Milo asked.
"I hope so," all the parents chimed in online. Together.

PAPA AND MAMA

BENI, EMMA, AND PENNY   SARA, HARRY, AND LIAM   GOLDIE, ABE, AND NOA   MOLLY AND SOPHIE

SAM, LUNA, AND BECKY   AVI AND MAX   ROSIE   GREAT-GRANDMA MINDEL

How do I get my camera to work? Help! Oy vey!

The next morning when Beni's family woke up,
the two candles were still burning. They cried out,
"A miracle happened here!" And, in a way, it did.

How to Make a Menorah

These menorah ideas are just for decoration and not to be lit. On a real menorah (chanukiah or hannukiah) a candle is lit for each of the nights to celebrate.

1. Find 8 small wooden or plastic spools empty of thread, and 1 large spool.
2. Cut oblong piece of wood or heavy-duty cardboard 1 ½ inches x 10 ¾ inches long.
3. Glue 9 spools in a row with the large spool in the middle (*shammash*).
4. Keep the spools the natural color or paint with glossy enamel or poster paint. (An adult should spray with varnish and leave windows open to let out any fumes.)

Penny's Menorah

1. Instead of spools, use ¾-inch circular wooden beads from a crafts supply store. Use blue and white beads, alternating the colors. For the *shammash*, put a white bead on top of a blue one to make it taller in the center of your menorah. Glue together.
2. Use self-hardening clay to make pretend candles to fit in the center hole of each bead. Roll different colors together to make swirled "candles."

MILO'S MENORAH

1. Paint 9 empty cardboard toilet paper rolls. Decorate with gold glitter.
2. Paste a clean Popsicle stick to the inside of each roll.
3. Attach a small piece of Velcro to one side of each stick.
4. Cut a "flame" out of yellow felt. Paste Velcro to one side of the flame. Attach to another "candle" for each night. Make 9.
5. Line them up. Glue onto a piece of oaktag, construction paper, or cardboard.

Note: With a felt-tip marker, Milo put a face on the felt flame he attached to the *shammash* candle!

LIAM'S MENORAH

1. In a small bowl, mix 1 cup flour, ½ cup salt, and ½ cup water. Knead together into a ball of dough, then divide in half.
2. Add 10 drops of blue food coloring to one ball and 10 drops of yellow to the other.
3. Knead both again. Divide each ball into 5 blue and 5 yellow balls.
4. Flatten bottoms. Line small balls flush up against each other in a row on a cookie sheet or flat baking pan, alternating colors. For the center *shammash* candle, put one color on top of the other. Rotate wax Chanukah candle in the center of each ball to create a hole in the dough.
5. Bake in 350 degrees Fahrenheit oven for about 30 minutes. Cool until hardened.
6. An adult can varnish the menorah.

"O Chanukah"

Moderato

Arr. Jonathan Zalben

O Cha - nu - kah, O Cha - nu - kah, come light the Me - no - rah.___
Oy Cha - nu - koh, Oy Cha - nu - koh, a yom - tov a shay - ner, a

Let's___ have a par - ty, we'll all dance the ho - rah.
lus - tig - er, a fray - lich - er, nit - du noch a zoi - ner,

Ga - ther 'round the ta - ble,
al - le nacht in drayd - lech___

you'll get a treat.
shpie - len___ mir,

Shi - ny tops to play with,
zi - dig hay se lat - kes

lat - kes to eat. And
est un a shir. Ge -

while we are
shvin - der tsint

play - ing, the
kin - der die

can - dles are burn - ing so bright.
din - in - ke lich - te - lach un.

One for each night, they___
Zugt al ha - ni - sim loibt

shed a sweet light, to re - mind us of days long a - go.
gott far die ni - sim un kumt gi - cher tant - zen in kon.

"I Have a Little Dreidel"

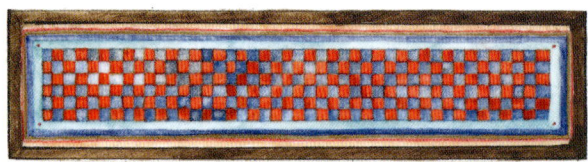

Arr. Jonathan Zalben
Folk Song Based on Lyrics by S. E. Goldfarb

Moderato

I have a lit — tle drei — del, I made it out of clay; And
It has a love — ly bo — dy, with legs so short and thin; And
My drei — del's al — ways play — ful, it loves to dance and spin; A

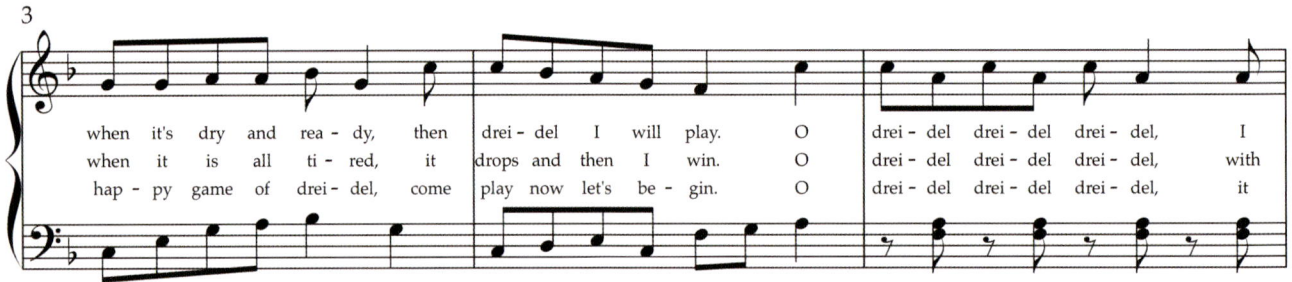

when it's dry and rea — dy, then drei — del I will play. O drei — del drei — del drei — del, I
when it is all ti — red, it drops and then I win. O drei — del drei — del drei — del, with
hap — py game of drei — del, come play now let's be — gin. O drei — del drei — del drei — del, it

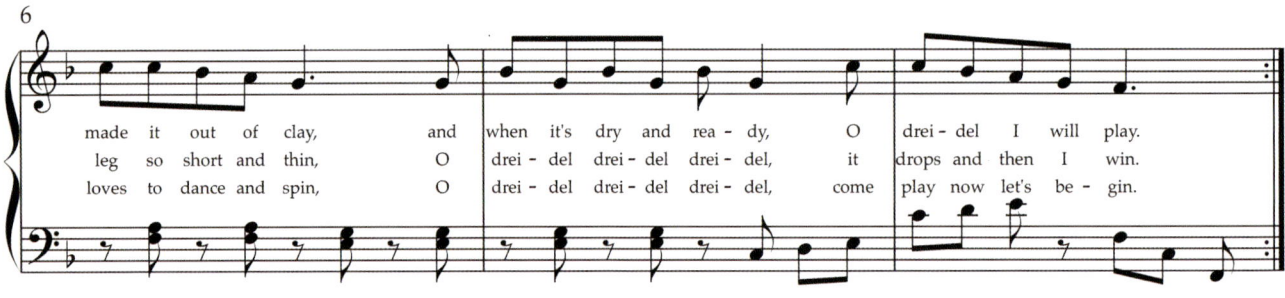

made it out of clay, and when it's dry and rea — dy, O drei — del I will play.
leg so short and thin, O drei — del drei — del drei — del, it drops and then I win.
loves to dance and spin, O drei — del drei — del drei — del, come play now let's be — gin.

HOW TO PLAY DREIDEL

A dreidel is a four-sided top usually made of wood or plastic, but it can also be clay, brass, or even glass. Over two thousand years ago, Jews were forbidden to study the Torah. So when soldiers passed by their homes, Jewish children would spin dreidels to hide that they were studying in secret. In Hebrew, a dreidel is called a sevivon *(spinning top). Each side is engraved with one of four Hebrew letters:* Nun, Gimmel, Hey, *and* Shin, *which stands for the phrase:* Nes Gadol Hayah Sham, *"A Great Miracle Happened There." In Israel,* Po, *which means "here," is substituted for* Sham.

1. Sit on the floor in a circle. Give each player an equal number of nuts, raisins, pennies, or chocolate candy coins wrapped in gold foil (*gelt*).
2. Each player places one item from their pile into the center—"the pot."
3. Take turns spinning the dreidel until it stops.
   If the dreidel lands on Nun, you get nothing.
   If it lands on Gimmel, you get everything.
   If it lands on Hey, you get half the pot.
   And if it lands on Shin, you have to put another item in the center.
4. When the pot becomes empty, each player has to put something in the center before the next spin, to start again.
5. The game is over when one player has everything.

(See below for Hebrew letters on each side of the dreidel.)

 Nun = nothing

 Gimmel = everything

 Hey = get half

 Shin = put back one. Players can chant, "Shin, shin, put one in!"

PAPA'S LATKES

Papa the "latke maven," known for his potato pancakes, won the latke contest last year when he made them Cajun-style.

4–5 large potatoes, peeled
1 medium onion, grated
2 large eggs, beaten

¼ cup matzoh meal
Pinch of salt and pepper
Oil for frying

1. Wash peeled potatoes in cold water. Grate finely.
2. Grate onion on larger side of grater, or in food processor.
3. Beat eggs. Add to mixture in large bowl.
4. Blend in matzoh meal, salt, and pepper.
5. Heat vegetable or olive oil in a large frying pan. Drop a heaping tablespoon of mixture into pan. When latke sizzles, turn over and fry until crisp and golden.
6. Drain on brown paper bag or paper towels.
7. Serve with applesauce or sour cream on the side.
   (Papa made a salsa and served that on the side.)

Yield: Serves about 6, depending on latke size and appetites (prime latke size is about 3 ½-inch round)

Note: You can substitute root vegetables for some of the potatoes, adding peeled and grated parsnip or turnips. Or add thin, small strips of zucchini (about ½ cup), ½ teaspoon dill, or thyme. Another idea: use sweet potatoes instead, with a pinch of red cayenne pepper for zing. Or add a sprinkle of paprika to regular potato mixture, using russets, Yukon golds, or Idaho potatoes. Make sure to drain liquid from vegetables in mixture so patties are firm when you fry them in the oil. (You can transfer latkes to a 250 degree-Fahrenheit oven to keep them warm until serving.)

APPLESAUCE

1. Put 8 large red baking apples, cored, in a baking pan.
2. Add 4 cinnamon sticks (bark), ½ cup raisins, 1 lemon (quartered), dark brown sugar to taste, a pinch of nutmeg or allspice, and a drizzle of maple syrup.
3. Simmer in oven at 350 degrees Fahrenheit until apples are soft and mushy.
4. Scoop out sauce from skins. Discard lemon wedges and bark.
5. In a large bowl, mash the applesauce mixture through a fine-mesh strainer or sieve. Or leave it as is: slightly chunky. Serve a dollop on top of each latke or on the side.

SWEET SALSA

3 tomatillos or 1 red pepper, diced

3–4 Campari tomatoes, diced
  (or a box of grape tomatoes cut in halves)

1 small red onion, peeled and diced

1 mango, peeled and diced
  (or 1 pear or ½ cup diced pineapple)

1 tablespoon lime juice

¼ cup apple cider vinegar

1 teaspoon brown sugar,
  dissolved in a bit of
  warm water (optional)

Pinch of salt (to taste)

Pinch of pepper (to taste)

Handful of cilantro, chopped

1. Wash and dice vegetables and fruit on cutting board. Set aside in bowl.
2. Add spices and liquid ingredients. Add cilantro. Stir with spoon.
3. Refrigerate until ready to serve as a side dish to the latkes!

BENI'S FAMILY RECIPE FOR DOUGHNUT HOLES

Sephardic Jews, originally from Spain and Portugal, eat sufganiyot *(jelly doughnuts), which are small balls of fried dough, instead of latkes.*

1 package dry yeast

¼ cup warm water

1 large egg, beaten

1 ¾ cups milk

1 stick of butter, softened

¾ cup granulated sugar

2 dashes of salt

Dash of nutmeg

Dash of cinnamon

Zest from 1 lemon

5 cups unbleached all-purpose flour, sifted

Large pot of oil for frying

Grape, raspberry, or strawberry jelly
   or jam preserves (optional)

Confectioner's sugar for dusting
   doughnut holes

1. In a small bowl, dissolve yeast in warm water for 10 minutes.
2. Add foamy yeast to beaten egg. Mix. Set aside.
3. Scald milk (heat milk on medium, stirring frequently, until it bubbles around the edge and gives off steam) in small saucepan. Add butter to hot milk. Cook until butter is melted. Remove from heat. Leave mixture until lukewarm. Add in sugar, salt, nutmeg, cinnamon, lemon zest, and yeast mixture.
4. Put mixture in large mixing bowl. Blend in flour. Knead until elastic ball of dough forms. Cover with dish towel. Set aside in warm area. Wait until dough doubles in size (2 hours). Remove dish towel. Punch down dough. Rip off pieces into nuggets smaller than walnut-size.
5. Dust fingers with flour to roll nuggets into balls. (Perfect task for a child.)
6. Pierce the center of ball with a skewer. Put a tiny bit of jelly inside each ball (doughnut hole). To seal, smooth dough over hole with warm water. (This step is optional. Beni's family dips the fried doughnut into jelly.)
7. Heat oil in pot. When bubbling, add a few balls at a time. Deep fry quickly (about 3 minutes, rolling ball around with ladle until lightly browned on all sides). Drain on paper towels on top of a plate.
8. Little hands can put the fried dough—a few at a time—in a paper lunch bag ¼ filled with confectioner's sugar and shake to coat the doughnut hole— *sufganiyot*. Repeat process until all the dough is used.

   Yield: About 3 ½ dozen (unless you eat them as you make them!)

DREIDEL AND MENORAH COOKIES

1 large egg yolk (reserve the egg white)
1 teaspoon vanilla extract
2 tablespoons orange juice
3 cups unbleached flour, sifted
1 cup granulated sugar

2 sticks softened butter
Long sprinkles for decorating
  as menorah candles
Crystallized sugar, blue and
  white for dreidels

1. In small bowl, beat egg yolk, vanilla, and orange juice together.
2. In large bowl, combine flour, sugar, and room-temperature butter.
3. Mix together. Knead until you form a ball of dough.
4. Refrigerate for 1 hour wrapped in waxed paper or plastic wrap.
5. Preheat oven to 350 degrees Fahrenheit. Grease cookie baking pans or line pans with parchment paper if you are not using nonstick pans.
6. Remove dough from waxed paper. Using a rolling pin, roll out dough on floured surface until it is as thin as possible without sticking.
7. Press cookie shapes into pastry dough. (Penny did a dreidel. Milo did a menorah. And Liam made both!)
8. Use a different color sprinkle to represent each candle on the menorah.
9. For dreidel cookies, glaze each cookie with reserved egg white, using a pastry brush or a clean new 1-inch-wide paintbrush. Sprinkle crystals to glitter on top of surface afterward.
10. Bake for 10 minutes or until a very slight golden edge is visible. Cool on rack.

Yield: 4 dozen, depending on size and shape

Note: One year, Beni poked a hole with a skewer in each cookie before they were baked. When they were done, and cooled, he inserted a silver thread or ribbon through each hole and hung them on a long string.

Tu B'Shevat

*In the Bible, the Tree of Life and the Tree of Knowledge
were planted in the Garden of Eden.*
(Genesis 2: 9)

Tu B'Shevat, the New Year of Trees, falls during winter, often in late January or early February, when trees form buds. In Jewish custom, a tree is planted when a baby is born. Both are cared for as they grow. The branches of a tree can be used as poles to hold up a *chuppa* (canopy) under which the grown child is married. This continues the cycle of life. The Torah, the first five books of the Jewish Bible, is referred to as the "Tree of Life."

There are symbols and stories in Judaism that refer to trees, linking the religion to the environment. The spirit of the holiday, the importance of being caretakers for the earth, is shown in the words of Solomon ibn Gabirol, a medieval Jewish poet in Spain, who most likely lived from c. 1020 to 1057: "The world is a tree, and human beings are its fruit."

The Tree of Life, as a metaphor for the Torah, comes from the Book of Proverbs, which uses the term three times. The most famous is: "*Etz chaim hee l'machazikim bah*" ("She is a tree of life to those who grasp her"), Proverbs 3:18, and is commonly sung as the Torah is returned to the ark.

TU B'SHEVAT SEDER PLATE

The seven fruits associated with Israel—olives, dates, figs, grapes, pomegranates, wheat, and barley—are eaten at a special Seder.

1. *Olives:* The hardy olive tree casts shade and provides fruit. It is a sign of hope. An olive branch is a symbol of peace.
2. *Dates:* The date palm is beautiful and strong with sweet fruit.
3. *Figs:* The Torah has been linked to the fig tree, a symbol of peace.
4. *Grapes:* Four cups of grape wine are sipped to represent the change in the four seasons. (Grape juice can be substituted.)
5. *Pomegranates:* The tough outer skin reminds us of the physical world that protects the softer spiritual world (inside the fruit). Also, the many seeds symbolize fertility and life.
6. *Wheat:* Bread is the staff of life.
7. *Barley:* The fruits of the soil.

MILO'S MAPLE MYSTERY

Beni said, "Would you like to have a nature adventure?"

"Sure," replied Milo. "Can Penny and Liam come?"

"The more the merrier."

So they also invited Noa, Sophie, and Baby Becky.

A frosty coating of snowflakes blanketed the woods.

Not a single leaf was on the trees, yet. *Trunks, roots, and branches are like skeletons with creepy extended arms*, thought Milo as he followed his father in the late-winter air.

Beni drilled a hole and hammered a spout into a maple tree and hung a pail.
"Nights are cold, but the days are becoming warmer."
Milo trembled as he watched the bucket fill with a clear oozing liquid
flowing out of the tree. "What's *that*?"
"The tree's blood! Boo!" Penny tried to scare him.
Milo wondered. *It looks like water.*
"It's called sap. You collect it and boil it—over hours and hours—until
it makes a small amount of maple syrup."
Beni gave each of them a taste. "It's sweet!" shouted Milo.
So Penny tried it. "Can I have a little more?" she asked.
"Me too," all the cousins chimed in, taking turns to taste.

As they watched the sap drip, Beni said, "Hundreds of years ago, Indigenous peoples celebrated the end of winter and the return of spring by giving thanks to the largest tree in the forest grove. They tapped trees and did ceremonial dances around fires. They dripped hot syrup onto snow to form 'wax sugar' candy. Legend has it, Iroquois tribes were the first to make maple syrup." When the sun began to fade and the temperature dipped, Milo and his family walked home.

Later, Beni made pancakes for dinner. With fresh maple syrup.
All warm and sticky and sweet. And life couldn't get any better.
"Mystery solved." Milo let out a breath as Beni tucked him into bed
that night. And together they gazed outside at the moon—which was
the color of maple syrup.

PAPA'S PANCAKES FOR DINNER

Papa, Beni and Sara's father, tapped maple trees for syrup when they were young, usually in February (the time of Tu B'Shevat) when the clear sap begins to flow out of the tree. He invited their friends over to boil down the sap into amber syrup, and when it was ready they had pancakes for dinner!

1 cup all-purpose or whole wheat flour
1 teaspoon baking powder
¼ teaspoon salt
1 cup milk

1 large egg, beaten
1 teaspoon plain yogurt
Mini chocolate chips or fruit
  of choice (optional)

1. In a large bowl, stir flour, baking powder, and salt with a fork.
2. Pour in milk, egg, and yogurt. Mix until batter is smooth.
3. Heat frying pan or griddle coated with oil or butter over medium heat.
4. Pour or spoon batter onto pan to make about a 4-inch round pancake. (Toss into batter a few blueberries, chocolate chips, or banana slices, if you'd like to add some other flavor to your pancakes.)
5. Cook until the surface of each pancake is speckled with tiny bubbles. Then flip over and cook the other side until lightly browned.
6. Serve with homemade or store-bought pure maple syrup on pancakes.

Yield: 7 pancakes (double the recipe if you have a large crowd)

Tree-Planting Celebrations Around the World

Tree planting is celebrated in many parts of the world and is an important custom in many religions. In the United States, Arbor Day falls on the last Friday of April. The date can vary from state to state throughout the nation due to planting conditions. The holiday began in 1972 in an effort to plant a million trees in the grasslands of Nebraska. Today, we also celebrate Earth Day on April 22 to honor our environment.

In Israel, white and pink almond blossoms bloom during Tu B'Shevat. There are cherry blossom festivals during spring in Asia, particularly in Japan, Korea, and China, where families picnic in parks. In Nepal, on the border between India and China, young girls are married to a small tree (*bel*). A "marriage tree" is common in southern India as a representation of an ancestor. *Van Mahotsav* is a weeklong tree-planting festival celebrated all over India. In various African cultures, trees mark the transition from childhood to adulthood. Among the Ndembu, the milk tree (*mudyi*) is used in rituals as a symbol of life and morals. There is a Tree Fest in Tunisia (northern Africa) and a Tree-Planting Day in Lesotho (southern Africa). Now, more than ever, there's a global effort to make our world better by being environmentally conscious. Trees improve our soil, our air, our wildlife, and our health. They help to fight climate change on our planet.

How to Grow a Maple Tree

Before you grow a sugar maple tree, you need a seed to plant. Usually, the maple seedpods blow in the wind and sprout in the garden during springtime. Papa had so many saplings, he had to pull some out of the ground because they were growing everywhere!

1. Collect maple seedpods in the fall.
2. Soak the seeds in water for 2 days at room temperature.
3. Plant a few seedpods 1 inch deep in a small flowerpot filled with peat moss and soil. (Or you can place them in a large plastic freezer bag. Cover seeds with soil.) This creates a tiny greenhouse filled with moisture.
4. Place on a sunny windowsill or hang bag near window.
5. Water a bit every day. Wait for seeds to sprout.
6. Once the seeds germinate, you can transplant them outside in the spring. Dig a hole about 3 inches deep. Put sprout in the hole. Fill the hole with dirt so your sapling stands upright. Create a small well around the base. Water.
7. Keep moist. Water twice a week. Watch it grow!

Note: Maple seeds develop in pairs on a stem. Each seed is attached to a papery wing-like structure. The seedpods fall from maple trees and whirl in the wind like helicopter blades. The cousins stick them on their noses and twirl in circles until they're so dizzy they fall onto a bed of soft moss and giggle, imagining the aroma of sweet syrup in the air.

BACKYARD MAPLE SYRUP

Beni helped the children identify sugar maple trees in their backyards—best for making syrup. And he did the work to set up tree tapping. A Cub Scout when he was little, Beni made a wood fire with logs in a wide-open area. One year, he did it in a large metal pan on the patio grill! And another, in a pot on the stove's top burner in the kitchen.

1. Watch as an adult drills a small hole in the maple tree trunk bark on the sunny side of the tree, where the sap flows during daytime hours. Sap will begin to ooze and flow!

2. Set spout snugly in hole at a slight angle, tapping lightly with a hammer. Place above snow line—not too low or too high.

3. Collect sap by hanging a covered metal pail or bucket. (Covered, to keep out rain, snow, twigs, bugs, etc.) A good tree may produce 20 quarts in a 12-hour period! Empty pail to collect sap before it freezes at night.

4. Strain sap with a baking sieve, strainer, or cheesecloth. (If sap looks clean, skip this step.)

5. Boil down sap over a fire. Use a metal pan or a disposable aluminum roasting pan.

6. Sap turns to syrup; syrup turns to candy! So watch it boil: 40 gallons of sap = 1 gallon of syrup! It takes lots of hard work. You will know it is done when it's the amber color of honey. Note: take a ladle, or a long-handled serving spoon, and lift some of the hot liquid. If it runs off the spoon in a stream it's not syrup yet. It's syrup when it falls in little sheets, or "aprons."

7. Filter syrup with cheesecloth or a coffee filter. (Use fresh cheesecloth or a new filter every 2–3 gallons.)

8. Sterilize jars in an extra-large pot of boiling water (like in the canning process).

9. Bottle syrup in a clean, tightly sealed glass jar. Store in a cool, dark place.

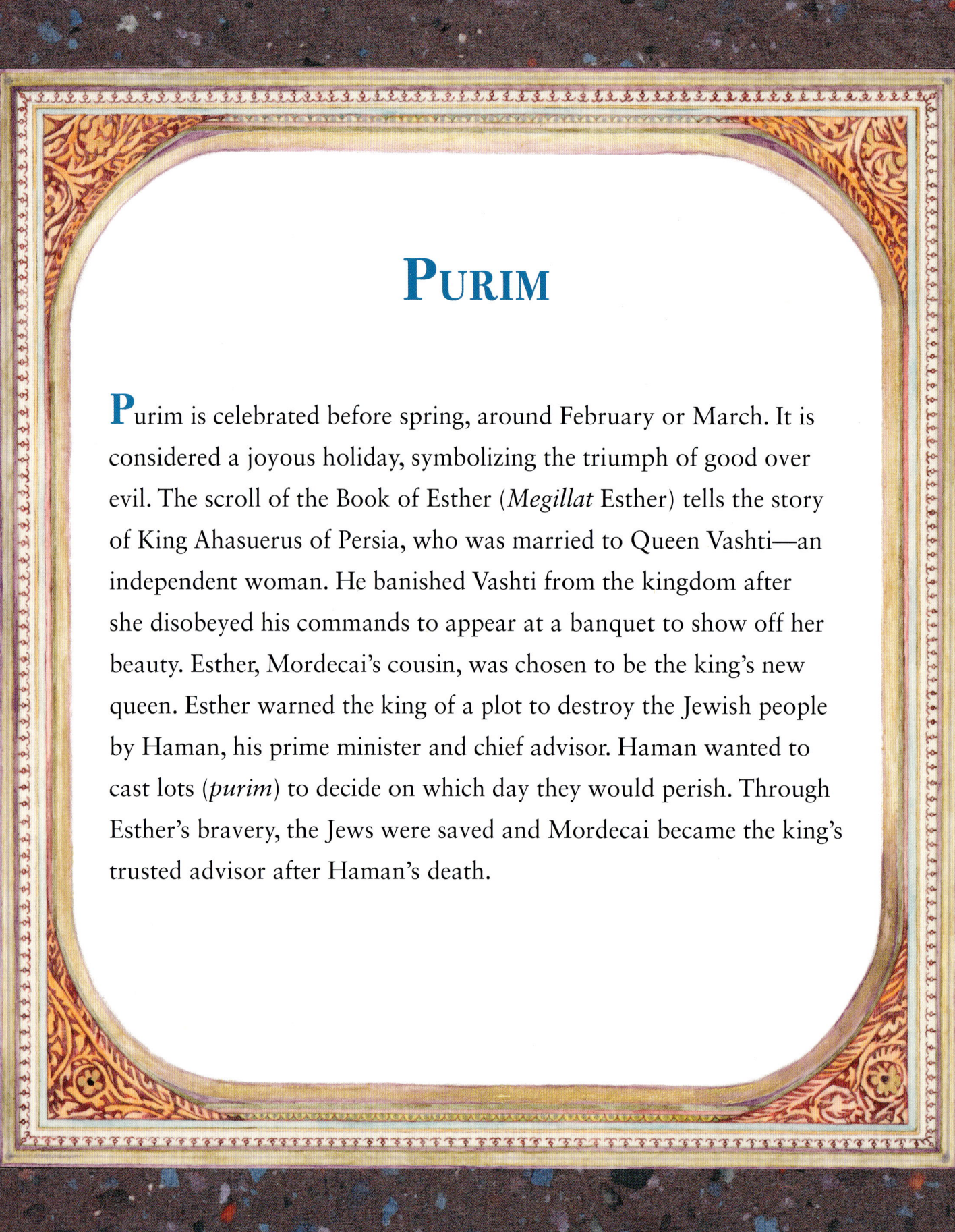

PURIM

Purim is celebrated before spring, around February or March. It is considered a joyous holiday, symbolizing the triumph of good over evil. The scroll of the Book of Esther (*Megillat* Esther) tells the story of King Ahasuerus of Persia, who was married to Queen Vashti—an independent woman. He banished Vashti from the kingdom after she disobeyed his commands to appear at a banquet to show off her beauty. Esther, Mordecai's cousin, was chosen to be the king's new queen. Esther warned the king of a plot to destroy the Jewish people by Haman, his prime minister and chief advisor. Haman wanted to cast lots (*purim*) to decide on which day they would perish. Through Esther's bravery, the Jews were saved and Mordecai became the king's trusted advisor after Haman's death.

MEGILLAH

The Scroll of Queen Esther

&

Mordecai the Jew

Goldie as Esther, Molly as Vashti, and Beni as Mordecai when they were children.

TWO STARS OF THE STORY

"**O**nce upon a time, I had a little cousin named Goldie, who played Queen Esther in the Purim spiel," said Beni.

"Guess who was King Ahasuerus? Ruler of the empire. Me!"

Goldie gave a long, exasperated sigh. "Not this again!"

"And she was *so-o* scared to say her lines in front of the entire congregation at the synagogue," her brother, Sam, continued. "I had to shout, 'Go, Esther!' when she couldn't speak or move."

"Thanks for reminding me," Goldie said. "As if I could *ever* forget."

"What happened next?" Cousin Noa glanced up at her mother.

"In the end, I was brave like Queen Esther," Goldie told Noa.

"I said my lines perfectly. And became Queen of Persia by telling the king about Haman's evil plot to destroy the Jews!" Goldie cried out. "*Esther* saved them!"

"Well," said Goldie's sister, Molly, "your part is not as brave as *my* part: the beautiful Queen Vashti." She flashed her famous smile, looking mischievous. Everyone turned toward Molly, a bit surprised, since Queen Esther had always been the star of the story. "When King Ahasuerus ordered Vashti to come to his palace because of her beauty, and she said, 'No!' and was then banished from the kingdom…wasn't *she* a heroine, too?" Goldie rolled her eyes at her sister.

"Both women were brave," Emma broke in.

"Two stars of the story."

Cousin Noa said, "Well, I'm going to be Queen Esther next year. Just like *my* mother." She glanced up toward Goldie.

"I'm going to be Queen Vashti next year. Just like *my* mother," said cousin Sophie as she glanced up at Molly.

Goldie and Molly agreed to disagree, each wanting to be the star of the story.

But their daughters, Noa and Sophie, realized they were both queens because Vashti was strong and Esther was wise.

They were brave in their own ways. And there's room for many stars in the sky as well as here on earth.

GOLDIE'S HAMANTASCHEN

Goldie said, "Over the years, I keep perfecting this recipe. Sometimes I change the dough. Sometimes, the filling. Whatever I do, the shape is the same: pastries folded into triangles known as 'Haman's pockets.'" (In Yiddish, taschn *means "pockets." Some think Haman wore a three-cornered hat or had pointy ears!) Hamantaschen, named after evil Haman, are given along with fruits, nuts, and chocolates in gift baskets (shalach manot, which means "sending portions") to friends, as Mordecai instructed the Jews to do on the first Purim celebration.*

DOUGH

2–2 ¼ cups all-purpose flour

3 ounces cream cheese, softened

2 teaspoons baking powder

½ cup butter, softened

Pinch of salt

½ teaspoon vanilla extract

⅔ cup sugar

2 tablespoons milk

¼ teaspoon cinnamon

2 tablespoons fresh orange juice

1 orange (grated rind for zest, and juice)

1 large egg

2 teaspoons orange zest in dough filling

Haman's Three-Cornered Hat

1. Sift flour and baking powder. Mix in salt, sugar, and cinnamon. Set aside.
2. In a mixer, cream together softened butter and cream cheese, adding grated zest from the orange peel. (Save inside of the orange for juice.)
3. Add vanilla, milk, orange juice, and egg to creamed mixture. Blend.
4. To form a soft dough, add dry ingredients to creamed ingredients.
5. Refrigerate dough for 3 hours or overnight.
6. Preheat oven to 350 degrees Fahrenheit.
7. Place dough on lightly floured board, table, or countertop surface. Roll out with rolling pin to flatten dough to about ⅛-inch thick.
8. Cut into 3-inch circles using an upside-down glass or round cookie cutter shape.
9. *Filling:* Fill each circle with ½ teaspoon: poppyseed-prune mixture; or apricot preserves or raspberry jam with mini chocolate chips or Nutella spread; or minced dates-walnuts-and-honey mixture with zest.
10. Press three sides of the circle, pinching together to form triangles. Smooth corners with your fingers dipped in water. Place hamantaschen (filling edge up) on a greased cookie sheet.
11. Bake for 10 minutes or until light tan in color.

Yield: About 3 dozen

Note: Dairy recipe. If pareve, substitute dairy-free cream cheese or silky tofu, water for milk, and margarine for butter.

HOW TO MAKE A PURIM MASK

Beni and Emma interrupted the hoopla and said to the kids, "In the playroom is 'stuff!' Go make costumes!" They discovered all sorts of dress-up clothing, fabric, beads, jewelry, and bangle bracelets to make outfits for a Purim spiel. Noa grabbed a scarf. Sophie a tiara. Becky sat in the middle, putting it all on her head.

"How cute is that?" said Sam as he picked up his baby daughter.

"We need masks!" suggested Liam, who was quite the budding artist along with Milo and the other cousins.

Materials: Paper plates, scissors, ribbon, paints, glitter, sticky gems, markers, crayons, feathers, glue, elastic thread, pipe cleaners

1. Cut a mask shape from half a paper plate. Draw space for eyes. Cut out holes to see. Set aside the bottom half and use it later if you want to draw a crown to attach to the mask.

2. Decorate mask with paints, glitter, feathers, sticky gems, markers, crayons. Be creative!

3. Measure ribbon (or elastic thread) along the back of your head. Add 12 inches. Cut length. Then cut in half to get two pieces.

4. Attach ribbon to mask by stapling or gluing each piece to the side of the mask so you can tie it into a bow and wear.
    Optional: Glue a thick, fuzzy colorful pipe cleaner to one side of the mask to hold in front of your face. Like a Mardi Gras mask!

HOW TO MAKE A GROGGER

Molly's motto is: "Make noise!" Clearly, she's the one to demonstrate how to make a grogger. When the scroll is opened to the story of Esther, every time wicked Haman's name is said during the reading of the megillah, everyone whirls their groggers in the air and stomps their feet, making a lot of noise that can be heard throughout the synagogue to blot out Haman's name. In this festive celebration, Molly is the loudest of all.

Materials: paper cups and small paper plates, clear packing (or duct) tape, empty cardboard toilet paper roll, small plastic bottle, or can, or jar, paints, construction or colored tissue paper, sequins, feathers, wooden tongue depressor, or chopsticks, glue, beans, dry noodles, popcorn kernels, pennies

1. Find an empty container to become a noisemaker. Here are some ideas: Use 1 paper cup (seal with a lid when it is filled), or staple together 2 small paper plates around the circumference (leave a small space to fill), or a cardboard toilet paper roll (later sealed at either end with tape), or a small can or plastic bottle, or a jar (save lid).
2. Decorate with paints, construction paper, or tissue paper, sequins, feathers, etc. For the holder (optional) glue a wooden tongue depressor or 2 chopsticks to your paper container.
3. Fill the inside of your container with popcorn kernels, a handful of beans, dry noodles, or some pennies. Anything you can think of that will make sound when you shake it.
4. Seal your container. Shake to make noise!

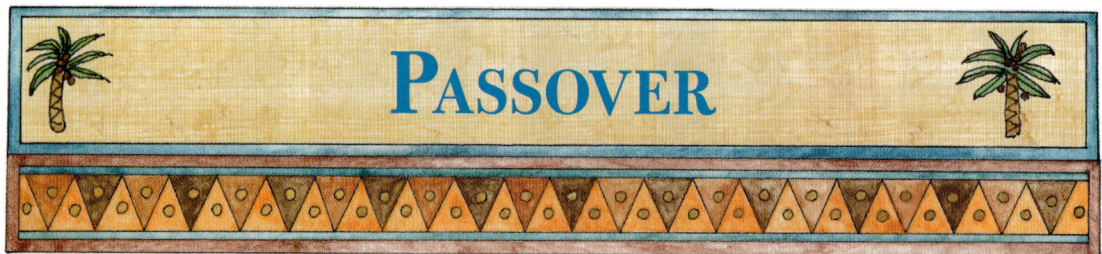

PASSOVER

Passover, the Festival of Freedom, commemorates the Exodus of the Israelites from slavery to freedom. It is usually celebrated in April, and lasts for eight days. Pharaoh, the ruler of Egypt, wouldn't give the enslaved Jewish people freedom, so God brought Ten Plagues upon the Egyptians. The Hebrew people were led by Moses out of Egypt. They left in such haste, their bread didn't have time to rise. Unleavened bread (*matzoh*) is eaten in remembrance. Matzoh represents the "bread of affliction." The *Seder*, which means "order," is a ritual family meal held the first two nights of the holiday, where customs are observed in a specific order while the Exodus story is told. The longest part of the Seder is the *Maggid*. Each person around the table takes a turn reading the narration from the *Haggadah*, which means "telling" in Hebrew, saying blessings and prayers, asking questions, telling stories from the Torah about the difficult journey of the Jewish people, and together, singing songs, ending with the saying for peace, "Next year in Jerusalem!"

 RDER OF THE SEDER

1.	קַדֵּשׁ	*Kadesh:* The First Kiddush over the Ritual Wine
2.	וּרְחַץ	*Urhatz:* Washing Hands
3.	כַּרְפַּס	*Karpas:* Fresh Greens Dipped in Salt Water
4.	יַחַץ	*Yaḥatz:* Breaking the Middle Matzoh in Half (*Afikomen*)
5.	מַגִּיד	*Maggid:* Telling the Story
6.	רָחְצָה	*Roḥtzah:* Washing Hands before Eating
7.	מוֹצִיא	*Motzi:* The Brakhah (Blessing) over the Bread
8.	מַצָּה	*Matzoh:* Blessing the Unleavened Bread
9.	מָרוֹר	*Maror:* Eating the Bitter Herb
10.	כּוֹרֵךְ	*Korekh:* The Hillel Sandwich (Bitter Herb/Haroset on Matzoh)
11.	שֻׁלְחָן עוֹרֵךְ	*Shulḥan Orekh:* Serving the Meal (Means "the set table" in Hebrew)
12.	צָפוּן	*Tzafun:* Eating the Hidden *Afikomen* (Dessert)
13.	בָּרֵךְ	*Barekh:* Prayers After the Meal
14.	הַלֵּל	*Hallel:* Songs ("Halleluyah" comes from the Hebrew *hallel*)
15.	נִרְצָה	*Nirtzah:* A Final Wish for Peace and "Next year in Jerusalem!"

PASSOVER PING-PONG

"The whole family is coming to our place for a Seder!"
Sara smiled as Liam ate the last cookie, which was big enough for four.

"What about Rosie? She always does it," said Liam.

"There's no room in her apartment for our growing family."

"Where are we all going to eat?" Liam's father looked around.

"Downstairs in the basement playroom," Sara answered.

"Seriously?" asked Harry.

"Seriously," said Sara. "On the Ping-Pong table."

Two days before the big day, Harry and Liam took off the net,
cleaned the table, and spread a tablecloth across the top.

"Can I help set the table for the first night?" asked Liam.

Sara and Harry nodded yes. Liam placed a *Haggadah* by each plate.
He put Papa's silver *Kiddush* cup by his, next to Mama's old Shabbat
candlesticks, with the Seder plate in the center and three matzohs
tucked inside a matzoh cover he had made by himself. Liam placed
parsley sprigs by a bowl he filled with salt water, near the apple,
walnut, and date *ḥaroset*.

"Great job, buddy!" his parents said together, *kvelling* with pride.

On the night of the Seder, everyone went downstairs and saw the Ping-Pong table covered with beautiful linen.

Rosie said, "This gives a whole new meaning to *who's serving?*"

The highlight was when Milo asked,

"Why is this night different from all other nights?"

Everyone's stomachs grumbled as they continued to read.

Liam's favorite parts were reciting the *Ten Plagues*, singing "*Dayenu*,"

searching for the *afikomen*, and opening the door for *Elijah*.

But the best part was when his mom finally ladled *matzoh balls* into

steamy soup bowls—with a huge ball floating in each one.

When Liam tried to cut his matzoh ball with a soup spoon, it went

right over the center of the Ping-Pong table—as if the net were still

there!—and splashed into Penny's bowl.

"It's like the parting of the Red Sea!" he cried out.

"That's some fluffy matzoh ball you made this year,"

Harry whispered to Sara. "It's got some bounce to it."

"What's your matzoh ball doing in my soup?" shouted Penny.

"The back float?" Liam said and laughed.

The jokes were endless. So Penny began to cry.

"Not funny! My new dress is ruined.

You're the eleventh plague!" she screamed at Liam.

Everyone got quiet, and the Seder suddenly stopped.

Penny glanced down at her soup bowl. "I take it back."

"Why is this night different from all other nights?" Milo repeated.

"Because…," his father replied, "I think you accidentally scored a winner."

The family laughed again. Then ate. At the end of the Seder, Harry said

to his son, "Liam, maybe you should take up tennis?"

Sara elbowed Harry gently. "Or pickleball?"

Beni said, "Next year at our place. Volleyball, anyone?"

CRAFT IDEAS TO DO BEFORE PASSOVER

The holiday begins the night before, when the family searches the house for chametz—remaining bread and food that cannot be eaten during Passover. Liam did a bread crumb hunt using a candle, a wooden spoon, and a feather to sweep away any crumbs. When he found the last cookie and ate it, Liam said, "Hey, I'm just trying to help!" Then, Liam made some craft projects to get ready for the holiday ahead of time.

MAKE YOUR OWN MATZOH COVER

Decorate two pieces of cloth large enough to cover your matzoh. Sew, glue, or staple edges together. Slip three pieces of matzoh inside your "envelope." The three matzohs represent the three tribes of Israel: Cohens, Levis, and Israelites. Before the meal begins, the middle *matzoh* is broken in half. One piece, called "the *afikomen*" (in Greek), is saved to be eaten at the end of the Seder. It is considered the dessert matzoh. The leader of the Seder wraps it in cloth and hides it, and the children search for it in the evening. The one who finds it gets a little gift. In Beni's family, all the cousins get something!

stitch or draw "matzoh" in Hebrew

CHOCOLATE MATZOH

Melt chocolate in a double boiler pot or microwave. Dip matzoh in chocolate to coat. Allow to cool on a metal rack or waxed paper in the refrigerator.
Optional: Sprinkle finely ground nuts—any kind—or colored sprinkles on top of matzoh before it cools.

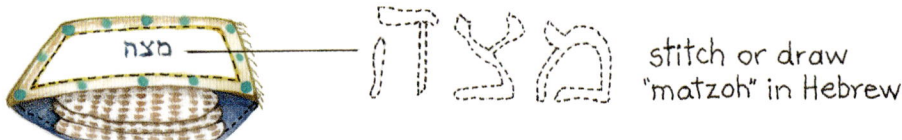

TEN PASSOVER PLAGUE PLACE CARDS

Fold an index card in half. Write each guest's name with gold or silver marker. Decorate with one of the Ten Plagues (such as kosher or coarse sea salt to represent hail glued with white glue or paste, or red nail polish for blood, or a tiny plastic frog). You can also draw symbols or main characters from the Exodus story, or fold origami animals!

ELIJAH'S OR MIRIAM'S CUP

Four cups of wine (or grape juice) are sipped during the Seder. A fifth goblet is for the Prophet Elijah. It's tradition to leave the front door open, hoping he will visit, drink from this cup, and bring peace on earth. The cousins watch this cup throughout the Seder, waiting for his arrival. A new feminist tradition includes Miriam's cup, filled with spring water. According to a *midrash* (story), Miriam, Moses's sister, led the women in song across the Red Sea and kept the Israelites alive for forty years during the Exodus with her magical well of water. Take a clear plastic drinking cup, decorate it, fill it with water, and put it in the center of the table alongside Elijah's cup.

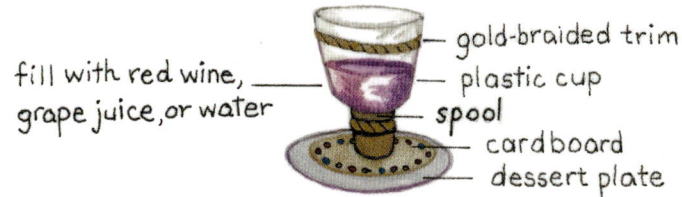

PENNY'S PLANS FOR A PASSOVER GARDEN PATCH

Passover reminds us of spring and rebirth as nature's buds burst. Mama, full of hope and excitement, planted herb and vegetable seeds in late winter (many she had dried and saved), including plants that are symbols on the Seder plate and those that are used for recipes in the meal.

This year, Papa built raised beds two feet by six feet long out of cedar wood planks. He surrounded them with ¼-inch cream-colored pea gravel and bricks along the walkway edges. Mama filled each oblong box with dirt from the compost heap (years of decomposed leaves, and kitchen scraps of rotted fruit, vegetable peels, eggshells, and coffee grounds). Then she added peat moss. You can use store-bought garden soil instead.

They drew a plan for a garden patch. All the cousins, except Baby Becky, who was napping, helped remove stones, weeds, and dried stems. Then they raked the beds. They put herbs like parsley, dill, thyme, rosemary, tarragon, and mint in boxes. Mama said, "I'd rather eat my plants than look at flowers. (Although the chives and sweet peas had gorgeous violet and pale pink flowers.) They did plant marigolds and nasturtiums to keep away insects.

PLANTING HERBS AND VEGETABLES

Mama, an avid gardener ever since she planted with her father when she was little, said, "I'm stepping up my game. Let's add root vegetables. They grow underground in the dark." Milo shouted, "Vampire vegetables! Garlic!" Mama smiled. "That's a good start." She suggested celeriac root (celery root), turnips, beets, horseradish, parsnips, and onions. One year, they tried fennel and asparagus with feathery fronds above ground like carrots. Then she added her usual crop of many varieties of tomatoes, peppers, lettuces, collards, leeks, peas, green beans, squash, cucumbers, eggplants, pumpkins, melons, and strawberries.

THE SEDER PLATE

The Passover Seder is the ritual meal. The Seder Plate has traditional food that represents different parts of the Exodus story. Use a plain white heavy-duty paper or plastic plate to make your own, drawing pictures of each symbol of food in crayons or markers. Or take a paper muffin cup and put food inside each one on the plate. Sara has a pretty plate from her mother—Mama—that she took out this year.

1. Egg (*beitzah*): The roasted egg is a symbol of life and fertility. It also recalls the time of sacrificial offerings in the Temple in Jerusalem.

2. Shank bone (*zeroa*): Burnt portion of lamb shank represents the paschal offering in memory of the ancient Temple sacrifice. (The year Max became a vegetarian, Cousin Rosie used a roasted beet instead.)

3. Bitter herbs (*maror*): Horseradish top. Some use romaine lettuce. It signifies the bitterness of slavery.

4. *Ḥaroset* (symbolizes "clay"): A fruit-and-nut mixture. (Chopped walnuts and apples for Ashkenazi Jews from Eastern Europe. Chopped dates and almonds for Sephardic Jews from Spain, Portugal, North Africa, or Middle Eastern countries.) It reminds us of the bricks and mortar the Israelites used to build pyramids when they were enslaved in Egypt. You can add cinnamon bark (sticks) to the plate to represent the strawless clay bricks the Israelites were forced to make. Red wine (or grape juice) in this mixture is a reminder that God parted the Red Sea during the Exodus when the Jews were led to freedom by Moses.

5. Parsley (*karpas*): The green herb reminds us of spring. Parsley dipped in salt water symbolizes the salty tears cried when the Israelites were enslaved.

6. Grated horseradish (*ḥazeret*): An additional bitter herb is eaten with the ḥaroset. This sweet paste tempers the bitterness of the maror in a small spicy matzoh sandwich bite (*korekh*)—that shows life has two sides: bitter and sweet.

THE FOUR QUESTIONS

The youngest child present asks:
Why is this night different from all other nights?

מַה נִּשְׁתַּנָּה הַלַּיְלָה הַזֶּה מִכָּל הַלֵּילוֹת.

–On all other nights we eat bread or matzoh:
Why tonight only matzoh?

שֶׁבְּכָל הַלֵּילוֹת אָנוּ אוֹכְלִין חָמֵץ וּמַצָּה
הַלַּיְלָה הַזֶּה, כֻּלּוֹ מַצָּה.

–On all other nights we eat any kind of herb:
Why tonight bitter herbs?

שֶׁבְּכָל־הַלֵּילוֹת, אָנוּ אוֹכְלִין שְׁאָר יְרָקוֹת
הַלַּיְלָה הַזֶּה מָרוֹר.

–On all other nights we don't dip the herbs even once:
Why tonight do we dip twice?

שֶׁבְּכָל־הַלֵּילוֹת, אֵין אָנוּ מַטְבִּילִין אֲפִלּוּ פַּעַם אֶחָת;
הַלַּיְלָה הַזֶּה, שְׁתֵּי פְעָמִים.

–On all other nights we eat either sitting or reclining:
Why tonight do we all recline?

שֶׁבְּכָל־הַלֵּילוֹת, אָנוּ אוֹכְלִין בֵּין יוֹשְׁבִין וּבֵין
מְסֻבִּין; הַלַּיְלָה הַזֶּה, כֻּלָּנוּ מְסֻבִּין.

Passover Songs Hit Parade

"Mah Nishtanah"
(Why Is This Night?)

Moderato

Arr. Jonathan Zalben

Mah nish-ta-nah ha- lai-lah ha-zeh mi- kol___ ha-lay- lot. mi- kol___ ha-lay-

lot?
1. She- b'- khol ha-lay- lot_____ a - nu okh-leen ha- metz___ u' ma-
2. She- b'- khol ha-lay- lot_____ a - nu ohk-leen sh' - ar_____ y' ra-
3. She- b'- khol ha-lay- lot ayn a - nu mat-bee-leen a - fee-lu pa'am e-
4. She- b'- khol ha-lay- lot_____ a - nu okh-leen bayn yosh-veen u -vayn m'su-

tzoh, ha- metz___ u' ma- tzoh. Ha - lai - lah ha-zeh ha-
kot, sh' - ar_____ y' ra- kot. Ha - lai - lah ha-zeh ha-
khat, a - fee-lu pa'am e- khat. Ha - lai - lah ha-zeh ha-
been, bayn yosh-veen u -vayn m'su- been. Ha - lai - lah ha-zeh ha-

lai - lah ha-zeh ku - lo ma - tzoh. Ha tzoh.
lai - lah ha-zeh ma - ror___ ma - ror.___ Ha mor.
lai - lah ha-zeh sh' - tay___ f' a - meem.___ Ha meem.
lai - lah hz-zeh ku - la - nu m'su- been.___ Ha been.

"*DAYENU*" (IT WOULD HAVE BEEN ENOUGH)

This ancient hymn thanks God for the miracles of the Exodus. Grandpa was the leader and read each line. Everybody chanted "Dayenu" together at the end of each phrase.

If God had taken us out of Egypt without punishing the Egyptians

It would have been enough for us. *Dayenu.* (Repeat after every line.)

If God had punished the Egyptians and not cast judgment on their gods . . .

If God had cast judgment on their gods and not slain their firstborn . . .

If God had slain their firstborn and not given us their riches . . .

If God had given us their riches and not divided the sea for us . . .

If God had divided the sea for us and now led us to dry land . . .

If God had not led us to dry land and drowned the Egyptians chasing us . . .

If God had drowned the Egyptians chasing us and not taken care of us in the
    desert forty years . . .

If God had not taken care of us in the desert forty years without feeding us manna . . .

If God had fed us manna without giving us the Sabbath . . .

If God had given us the Sabbath without bringing us to Mount Sinai . . .

If God had brought us to Mount Sinai without giving us the Torah . . .

If God had given us the Torah and not brought us into the land of Israel . . .

If God had brought us into the land of Israel without building us the Temple . . .

It would have been enough for us. *Dayenu.*

"DAYENU"

Allegro

Arr. Jonathan Zalben

Ee - lu ho - tzi, ho - tzi - a - nu, ho - tzi - a - nu mi - mitz - ra - yim. Ho - tzi - a nu, mi mitz - ra - yim, da - ye - nu.

Da - da - ye - nu, Da - da - ye - nu, da - da - ye - nu, da -

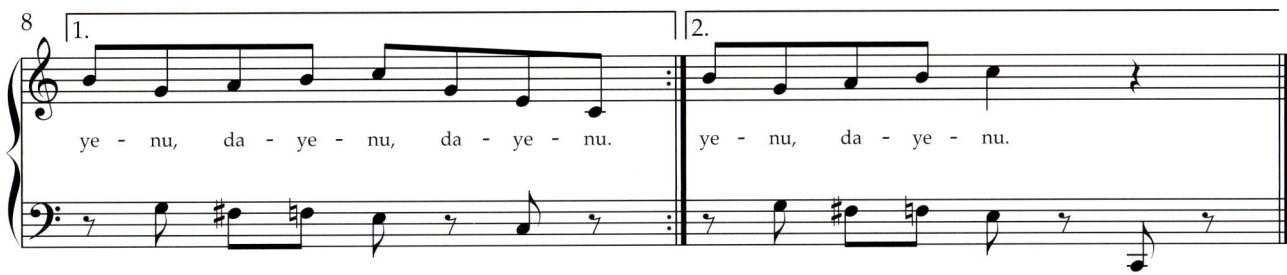

1.
ye - nu, da - ye - nu, da - ye - nu.

2.
ye - nu, da - ye - nu.

"CHAD GADYA" (ONE LITTLE GOAT)

One little goat, one little goat,
That my father bought for two *zuzim*.
Chad Gadya.

Then came the Angel of Death who killed
the butcher
Who slew the ox . . .

Then came the cat that ate the goat
That my father bought for two *zuzim*.
Chad Gadya.

Then came the Holy One, Blessed be God
Who killed the Angel of Death
Who killed the butcher
Who slew the ox

Then came the dog that bit the cat
That ate the goat . . . (*continue verse*)

That drank the water
That put out the fire
That burned the stick

Then came the stick that beat the dog
That bit the cat
That ate the goat . . . (*etc.*)

That beat the dog
That bit the cat
That ate the goat
That my father bought for two *zuzim*.
Chad Gadya!

Then came the fire that burned the stick
That beat the dog
That bit the cat . . . (*and continue verses*)

Then came the water that put out the fire
That burned the stick . . .

Then came the ox that drank the water
That put out the fire . . .

Then came the butcher who slew the ox
That drank the water . . .

"CHAD GADYA"

This song is fun to sing at the end of the Passover Seder. It is thought to be an allegory. Israel is "the kid," or little goat, bought by God for two zuzim (the two tablets of the Ten Commandments, or Moses and Aaron, who led the Exodus from Egypt). All the animals in the song symbolize the appearance of Israel's enemies, as well as their disappearance. Pharaoh had a dream of a scale. On one side of the balance were the people of Mitzrayim. On the other lay a "young kid." He feared from this dream that a child of Israel would be born who would lead his people to freedom. The ending of "Chad Gadya" is one of joy and overcoming oppression.

THE TEN PLAGUES

1. *Dahm:* Blood
   דָּם

   For one week, God turned the waters of the Nile—the source of food and drink—into a river of blood. Fish died; the river became foul. Only the land of Goshen, where the Israelites lived, had water.

2. *Tzfardeh-ah:* Frogs
   צְפַרְדֵּעַ

   Pharaoh would not let Moses's people go. So God said, "Tell your brother Aaron, 'Stretch your hand with a rod over the rivers, canals, and pools, and cause frogs to rise over Egypt.'" Frogs were in rivers, houses, beds, ovens, kneading bowls—everywhere—covering the land of Egypt. Pharaoh still refused.

3. *Ki-nim:* Lice
   כִּנִּים

   So Aaron stretched his rod into the earth's dust. Lice bit man and beast. Pharaoh's own magicians could not help. They said, "This must be a sign of God's presence." The Lord told Moses, "Rise up in the morning, go to Pharaoh, tell him to let my people go." Pharaoh still wouldn't listen.

4. *Arov:* Bugs
   עָרֹב

   The scarab, or beetle, was the sacred emblem of the Egyptian Sun god. It was sculpted on monuments and tombs, engraved on gems and amulets, and honored in all Egyptian images. God said, "Goshen will be set apart from the rest of Egypt. You will stand on the border looking toward Egypt and see swarms of bugs. In Goshen, there will be none." Pharaoh continued to ignore God's request to let the Israelites go.

5. *Dever:* Pestilence
   דֶּבֶר

   Then the Egyptians' cattle, horses, donkeys, and camels died, while herds and flocks in Israel lived. Pharaoh continued to say no, and the Israelites remained in slavery.

Everyone dips their pinky into a glass of wine (or grape juice), drops the droplet onto a plate, while saying together the name of each plague. Mama and Papa cry out, "Don't lick your pinky" (so no one symbolically swallows a plague)!

6. *Sh'hin:* Boils
שְׁחִין

Moses threw soot toward the heavens in sight of Pharaoh. The fine dust caused boils on people and animals. Even Pharaoh's magicians were unable to imitate what he did. Again, the Jews were spared.

7. *Barad:* Hail
בָּרָד

The Lord told Moses, "Hold your rod toward the sky." Hail fell across "every herb in the field." Lightning caused fires, killing everything in their path. When the rain, hail, and thunder ended, Pharaoh remained unmoved.

8. *Ar-beh:* Locusts
אַרְבֶּה

The land of Goshen continued to be spared, while locusts swarmed Egypt, eating crops. Egypt became a wasteland. Pharaoh's servants pleaded with him, "Let the Israelites go." But he didn't.

9. *Hoshekh:* Darkness
חֹשֶׁךְ

A heavy cloud hung over the land, hiding the sun. But the children of Israel had light in their homes. Finally, Pharaoh said, "Go. But your herds and flocks stay." He realized they would not leave their animals, so Pharaoh took back his offer. Moses replied, "I will not return to Egypt."

10. *Makat B'horot:* Death of Firstborn
מַכַּת בְּכוֹרוֹת

God told Moses: "There will be one last plague. A cry in the land of Egypt unlike any other." Moses told the people, "At dusk, mark your doorposts. That night, eat unleavened bread and bitter herbs. Anything left in the morning, burn. Eat in haste. (This was the first Passover Seder.) God will go through the land of Egypt and kill the firstborn of man and beast. The marked homes will be passed over by the Angel of Death. Eat unleavened bread for seven days and observe this feast for generations to come."

APPLE-AND-WALNUT HAROSET (*ASHKENAZI*)

4 cups shelled walnuts, chopped

5 cups sweet apples, peeled and chopped

Zest from 1 Meyer lemon, finely grated

1 teaspoon dark brown or granulated sugar

¼ teaspoon ground nutmeg

1¼ teaspoons ground cinnamon

½ cup Concord grape wine

2 tablespoons maple syrup

Handful of dried cranberries (optional)

1. Mix ingredients together in a food processor or by hand with an old-fashioned mortar and pestle.
2. Put in bowl. Cover. Chill before serving. Use at the Seder.
3. During the Seder, spread on small bite-size pieces of broken matzoh.

Yield: Enough for 30 or so guests, depending on who goes for seconds!

DATE-AND-ALMOND HAROSET (*SEPHARDIC*)

3 cups pitted dates, chopped

1 cup blanched almonds, chopped

1 teaspoon orange zest, finely grated

1 tablespoon fresh orange juice

Grated rind of 1 Meyer lemon for zest

½ teaspoon lemon juice

Pinch of nutmeg, ginger, or allspice

Pinch of cayenne pepper (optional)

¼ cup sweet or dry red wine

1 teaspoon of pomegranate juice

¼ teaspoon ground coriander or cardamom (optional)

Romaine lettuce leaves, washed (haroset served wrapped in lettuce)

1. In a food processor, chop nuts. Then blend to combine all the ingredients together to form a sticky paste.
2. Roll solid "paste" mixture with your hands back and forth on waxed paper to make approximately a 1½-inch-thick snake-like rope. Wrap in the waxed paper or plastic wrap to cool overnight in refrigerator.
3. On the day of the Seder, rope into ½-inch slices and wrap each slice in a small piece of lettuce leaf to give each guest a bite-size taste.

Yield: Around 25–30. This is favored in Middle Eastern countries instead of matzoh.

PLAIN AND BEET HORSERADISH

Horseradish paste is made for the bitter herb. Open windows while making it.
Liam's eyes teared up when his parents forgot to air out the kitchen! They made it
the day before the holiday to keep it fresh and ease the load of so much cooking.

3–4 medium-sized beets, boiled, peeled, and shredded (or canned beets)
2 ½ cups white vinegar (enough for soaking beets)
1 very large horseradish, peeled and julienned lengthwise to ⅛-inch-thick strips

1. Boil beets until soft. (Pierce beet to test softness.) Peel. Drain. Quarter. And then soak in 2 cups of white vinegar and refrigerate.

2. Peel horseradish. In food processor, finely grate or julienne. Put in bowl. Set aside. Add enough vinegar (around ½ cup) to make a horseradish paste. This makes about 6 cups. Separate (3 cups in each bowl) to make two different kinds: plain horseradish and beet horseradish.

3. For beet horseradish, drain the vinegar from the soaked beets, shred the beets in a food processor or julienne, and add beets to 3 cups of plain horseradish. Mix together. This type (½ cup drained beets per 1 cup horseradish paste) is less "authentic" because it's sweeter. During the Seder, spread on small pieces of broken matzoh (*maror*) sandwich. (You can also use as a side to gefilte fish.)

CELERIAC REMOULADE

Beni's family prefers this root vegetable with their gefilte fish instead of horseradish.

1 large celeriac root, peeled, cut in eighths, julienned to ⅛-inch matchsticks
3 heaping tablespoons mayonnaise (or to taste)
1 heaping tablespoon spicy brown mustard (or to taste)
½ cup white vinegar   Handful of fresh tarragon, finely chopped

1. Pulse in a food processor on medium or julienne by hand, shredding celeriac into approximately 1/8-inch-thick strips (like matchsticks).

2. Put celeriac aside in large bowl. Mix in other ingredients. Chill overnight.

GREAT-GRANDMA MINDEL'S CHICKEN MATZOH BALL SOUP

Sara doesn't use chicken fat (schmaltz) in her matzoh balls (kneidlach). She makes the soup, puts it in the freezer for a bit, and then skims off the solidified layer of fat because her great-grandmother Mindel said, "Go heart healthy. I'm aiming for one hundred! And no kneidlach is going to stop me." They made Mindel's recipe together at her home the day before the Seder.

1 large chicken (about 4–5 pounds)	1 parsnip, peeled and sliced
1–2 large carrots, peeled, sliced ½-inch thick	Pinch of salt (optional)
1–2 celery stalks with leaves	2 sprigs of fresh dill or parsley

1. Put chicken in an 8-quart pot and fill with enough water to cover the chicken until totally submerged.
2. Add carrots, celery, parsnip, salt, fresh dill (or 1 tablespoon dry dill). Cover pot. Simmer for around 2 hours or until the water is yellow. The chicken meat should be tender—almost falling off the bone.
3. Drain and remove vegetables and chicken from soup. Set aside. (Debone and skin chicken in a separate bowl so there is just the meat.)
4. Make matzoh balls (see recipe next page). Add to soup, cover, and simmer. (Some cooks like to make them separately in a pot of boiling water. Either way works. Mindel cooks them directly in her soup. Watch them grow (double in size).

Yield: 8–10 portions depending on the appetite and size of bowl

Note: In each bowl, Sara adds some chicken and vegetables with 1–2 matzoh balls, depending on size. She puts a piece of fresh parsley or fresh dill on top of each bowl. Except for Milo's! "No greens, please!"

Vegetarian soup stock: Follow the recipe above, except leave out the chicken. Add: 1 tablespoon olive oil, 2 sprigs of thyme, 2 bay leaves, 1 large onion (peeled and quartered), 1 white base of large leek (quartered lengthwise), 8 garlic cloves (peeled), 4 cardamom seedpods, and salt and pepper to taste.

MATZOH BALLS

The key to a fluffy matzoh ball is seltzer. As Liam discovered, it gives it that bounce! No one wants one that sinks to the bottom of a bowl. One year, Sara forgot the seltzer. They were as heavy as bowling balls. Boy, did she strike out!

4 large eggs, beaten

Pinch of salt

¼ cup olive or vegetable oil

1 cup matzoh meal

1 tablespoon chicken soup

2 tablespoons plain seltzer or club soda

Tiny pinch of ground pepper (optional)

Fresh parsley or dill sprig (garnish)

1. In medium bowl, beat eggs with salt and oil.
2. Pour in matzoh meal. Add chicken soup. Mix by hand with fork.
3. Stir in seltzer and continue to mix gently while it foams.
4. Cover and refrigerate for 1 hour. Remove.
5. Form into small balls somewhere between a walnut and Ping-Pong ball size. Before rolling each ball, dip fingers into cold water to moisten and make sure each matzoh ball is smooth and less sticky.
6. One by one, drop each matzoh ball into a large pot of boiling water or pot of chicken soup. Cover with lid. Reduce heat to simmer for about 20 to 30 minutes. Watch them grow bigger in size!

Yield: About 12 matzoh balls, depending on size (serves 6–8)

SMOKY BRISKET

Liam's father, Harry, has a hankering for brisket on Shabbat, Rosh Hashanah, and well, just about any time, but especially on Passover. His secret is adding tomatillos to give it a little zing! Milo also gave Liam maple syrup they had tapped on Tu B'Shevat as a shalach manot *gift during Purim, and Liam added it to this recipe!*

One first-cut kosher beef brisket, 6 or more pounds

6 Campari tomatoes (or any medium-sized tomatoes)

2 tomatillos (peel the outer paper)

8 ounces ketchup (or tomato paste)

2 tablespoons grape or black currant jelly

1 tablespoon maple syrup

1 cup sweet red wine (optional, but preferable)

¼ teaspoon smoke oil (optional—check kosher for Passover)

1 small onion, peeled and quartered

6 garlic cloves, peeled and chopped

7 bay leaves

1 large celery stalk cut into 1-inch slices

3 carrots, peeled and cut into 1-inch slices

Sprig of Italian parsley, finely chopped

Pinch of paprika (and tiny pinch of pepper and salt, optional)

15 baby new potatoes, or baby Yukon golds, or red ones, unpeeled

1. Put brisket in large, deep pot on stovetop. Add all ingredients except celery, carrots, and potatoes. (Set aside.)

2. Cover with lid. Cook for at least 2 hours. Remove brisket from pot. Place on cutting board. Slice against grain of meat into thin horizontal strips. Return meat to pot in sauce, adding celery, carrots, and potatoes.

3. Cover and continue to cook meat until tender and soft. (Or you can put all of this in a covered pan inside the oven at 350 degrees Fahrenheit along with the vegetables, cooking them until they are soft. Keep warm until serving.) *Harry once roasted the potatoes and carrots separately with olive oil and rosemary, and it was delicious for the vegetarians at the Seder!*

Yield: About 8–10 good eaters

BENI'S BROWNIES

1 stick (½ cup) unsalted butter or margarine

7 ounces semisweet chocolate

4 large eggs, room temperature

Pinch of salt

1 teaspoon vanilla extract

½ cup granulated sugar

¼ cup Passover cake meal, sifted

¼ cup bittersweet chocolate chips

¼ cup crushed walnuts (optional)

Confectioner's sugar for dusting

1. Preheat oven to 325 degrees Fahrenheit.
2. Grease an 8-inch square baking pan.
3. In a small pot on the stovetop, over a pan of simmering water, melt butter and semisweet chocolate. Stir until melted.
4. Remove chocolate mixture from heat. Cool to room temperature.
5. In a large bowl, beat eggs and salt (about 2 minutes). Add vanilla. Gradually add in sugar.
6. Whisk in the warm chocolate mixture.
7. Fold in sifted cake meal. (Sifting aerates the batter.) Beat until smooth.
8. Mix gently with bittersweet chocolate chips and crushed walnuts.
9. Pour into prepared pan. Bake for 30–35 minutes or until top is crusty.
10. Cool. Cut into squares. Dust with confectioner's sugar before serving.

Yield: 12 flourless brownies (Serve with dairy-free raspberry sorbet.)

Note: Passover cake meal is different from matzoh meal and is substituted for cake flour during Pesach. To make it kosher, you can replace the butter with pareve margarine if you are serving meat as part of the meal.

LAG B'OMER

Lag B'Omer is a festive holiday. It takes place in May, on the thirty-third (*lag* means "thirty-three" in Hebrew) day of the Counting of the Omer (*S'firat Ha'Omer*). This is the time *between* Passover and Shavuot, starting with the second night of Passover to the beginning of Shavuot (49 days) and symbolizes physical and spiritual freedom.

Rabbi Akiva's name is linked to Lag B'Omer. He lived during the time of the destruction of the Second Temple. The Romans forbid the study of the Torah, but he had become a great teacher and had thousands of students. Lag B'Omer is the day that marks the end of a mourning period of a plague that killed the rabbi's followers.

The festival is always celebrated with a large picnic. And in Israel, with bonfires, parades, playing bow-and-arrow, ball games, or a boy's first haircut at the age of three. Sometimes with weddings, too!

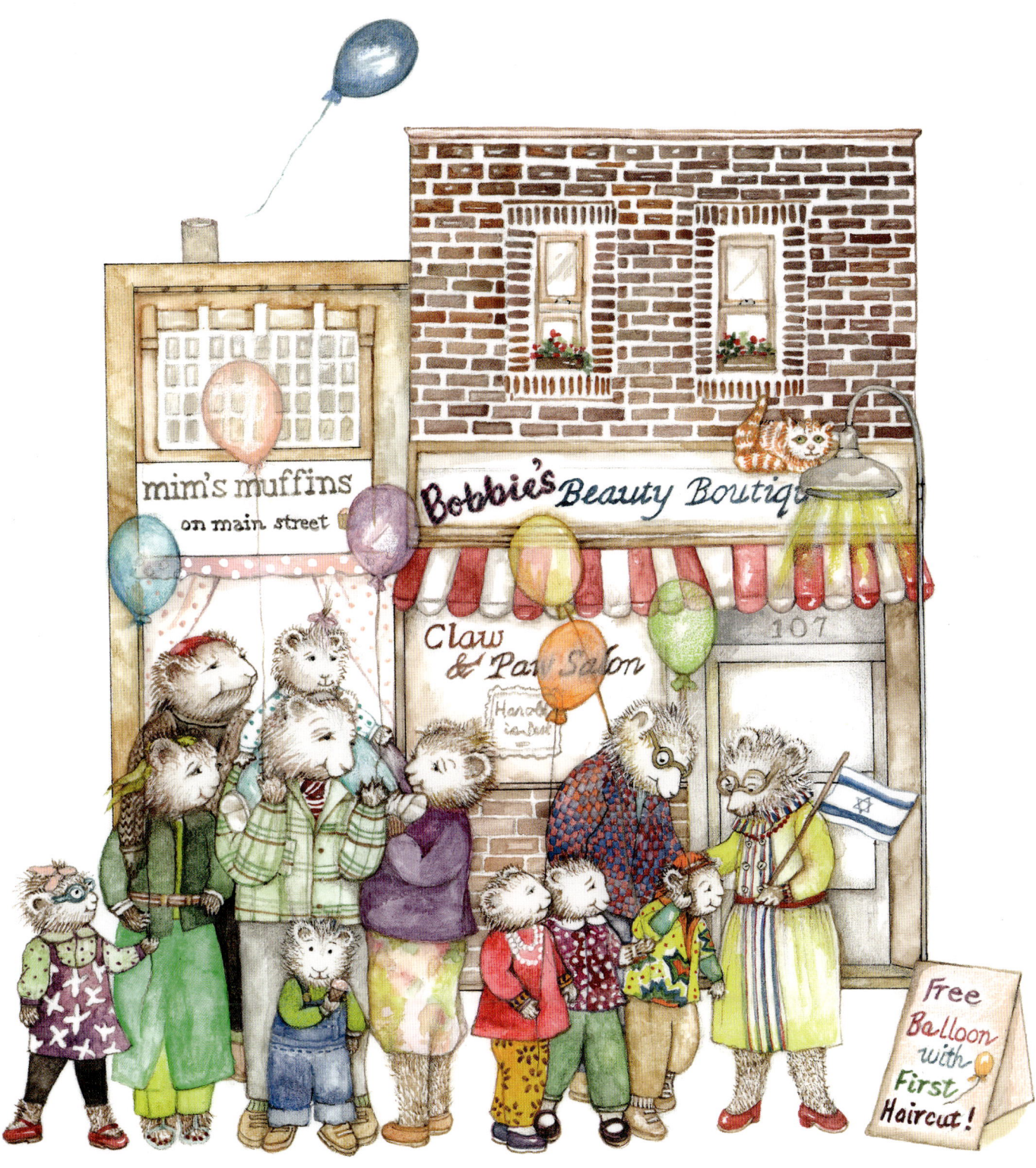

Penny's Picnic Party

Papa said, "It's Lag B'Omer. Let's all go to the park."

Penny asked, "Could we have a picnic?"

Milo chimed in, "And play baseball? I'm up first."

Liam said, "What about a bow-and-arrow battle?"

Noa declared, "I'm going to a parade."

Sophie added, "Can I come?"

Baby Becky just babbled, gurgling bubbles of spit.

The only words she knew were "Da. Da. Up. Go."

Cousin Sam smiled. "Becky's having her first haircut."

"I thought that was only for boys on Lag B'Omer?" Milo asked.

"Well, my little girl is getting hers," Sam said proudly.

First, they saw Becky get her bangs trimmed.

It was done with a pair of scissors from the craft box.

A new silk purple ribbon was tied around Becky's one curl.

Each cousin got a big balloon for being so patient.

And so did Becky, who didn't cry or wiggle.

Next, they went to a parade, and then had a baseball game.

Afterward, they did a battle with pretend bows and arrows.

And had a large picnic under an old weeping willow tree.

As usual, after so much food, the cousins napped.

At night in the moonlight, they went down to the lake in the park where there was a bonfire on the shore with singing and dancing. And then there was a wonderful surprise.

Beni took out a bag of marshmallows, bits of chocolate, peanut butter, and graham crackers, and said, "Go find twigs."

Then Papa roasted s'mores, and Mama, hot dogs, while Beni told them another tale. "Once upon a time, there was a Rabbi Akiva. Roman rulers forbid him to read the Torah. He was forced to flee for his life and spent twelve long years with his son studying in a cave."

"Was it dark?" Milo glanced over his shoulder. "Like here?"

Beni put his arm around Milo and continued the story:

"There was a miraculous well outside this cave."

"Oh," said Penny, "like Miriam's well? Was it magical?"

"I guess so," said Beni. "And also a carob tree. Like cocoa."

They listened as they all nibbled on chocolate s'mores.

"The well and the tree kept them alive for many long years. A plague raged amongst the rabbi's followers. Lag B'Omer celebrates the end of the plague."

"It does feel a little like Passover: plagues, wells, miracles. I'd like to explore a hidden cave someday," said Liam.

Milo shivered. "Not me." He asked for seconds on s'mores.

"This was the best barbecue picnic party ever," Penny said.

"I wish I could bottle today to remember it," sighed Beni.

"You'll remember it here." Mama pointed toward his head.

"And here." She pointed toward his heart. "And so will I."

S'MORES

This is a simple favorite around a campfire. Everyone cried, "Some more!" Papa did all the toasting over the fire while the cousins listened to Beni's tale.

---

1 bag marshmallows
1 large bar of chocolate or jar of Nutella
  (or chocolate chips)

1 jar peanut butter (optional)
1 box graham crackers

1. Pierce center of a marshmallow with tip of a very long twig or skewer. Rotate over the grill or fire and remove when toasted and drooping.

2. Place marshmallow between two graham crackers, adding broken bits of your chocolate bar inside. (Or use chocolate chips.)

3. Add peanut butter inside for the less traditional s'more!

4. If you want it super gooey, an adult should heat a "s'more sandwich" over the fire using very long tongs until the chocolate-marshmallow-peanut-butter combo oozes out the sides.

5. For a variation, place roasted marshmallow on chocolate-covered graham cracker smeared with or without peanut butter. Or add caramel. Once, Beni also added a bit of raspberry preserves to the chocolate/marshallow duo. It was a hit.

Note: S'mores are great with a glass of milk! Or even iced tea and lemonade.

COUNTING WITH COLORFUL CLOTHESPINS

Take 33 wooden clothespins. Paint each one a different color. With thin colorful markers you can add polka dots, stripes, or squiggles to wooden or plastic clothespins. String up inside or outside on a clothesline, and add a clothespin every day until you have 33 days!

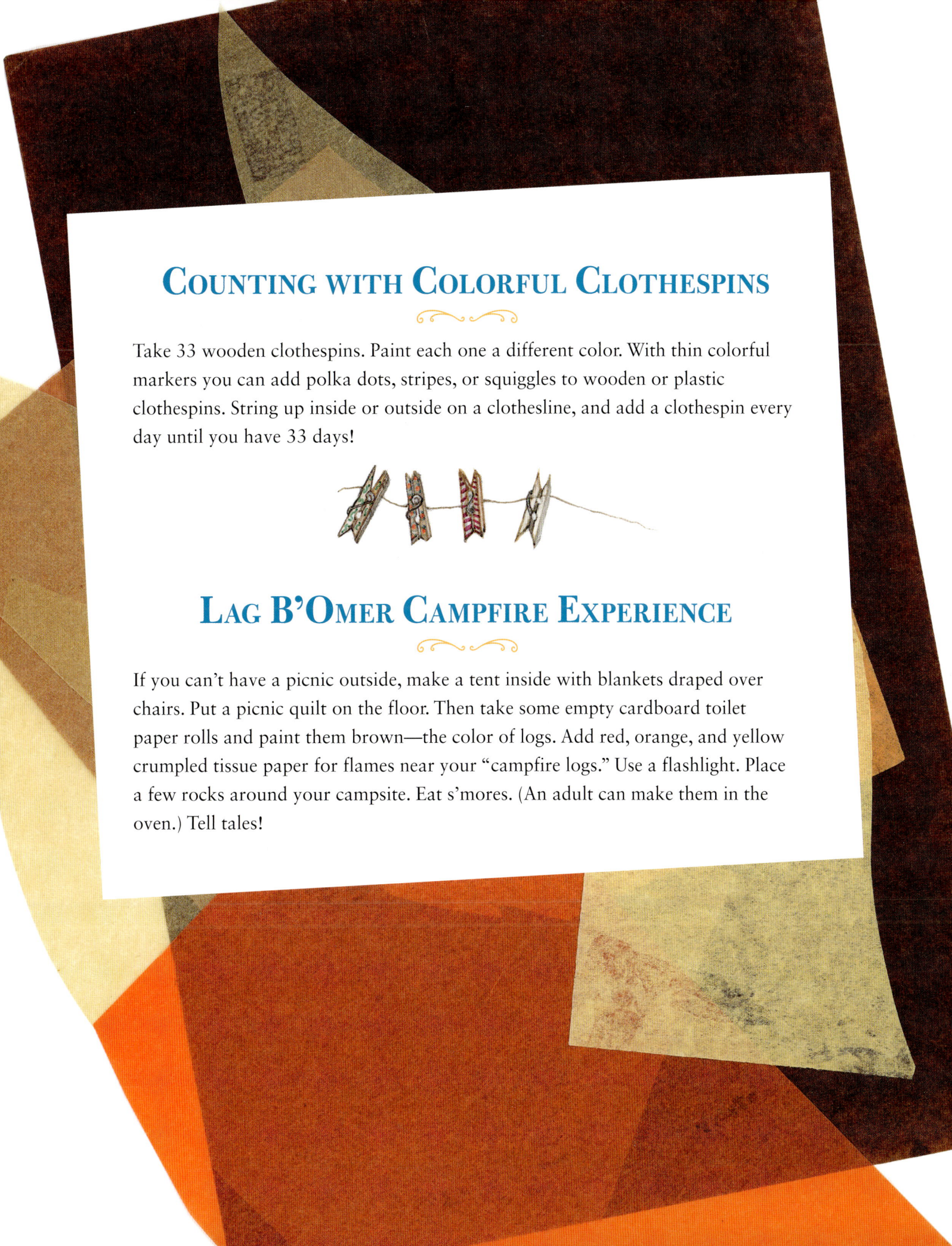

LAG B'OMER CAMPFIRE EXPERIENCE

If you can't have a picnic outside, make a tent inside with blankets draped over chairs. Put a picnic quilt on the floor. Then take some empty cardboard toilet paper rolls and paint them brown—the color of logs. Add red, orange, and yellow crumpled tissue paper for flames near your "campfire logs." Use a flashlight. Place a few rocks around your campsite. Eat s'mores. (An adult can make them in the oven.) Tell tales!

SHAVUOT

"He gave us this land, a land of milk and honey.
Where I now bring the first fruits of the soil."
Deuteronomy 26: 9–10

Shavuot is a wheat harvest, called the Feast of Weeks or the Festival of First Fruits, occurring in June. It celebrates the section in the Ten Commandments (a part of the Torah—the first five books of the Bible) where the Torah is given to the people of Israel on Mount Sinai after their freedom from slavery in Egypt. The festival lasts two days. On the second day, the Book of Ruth, one of the five biblical scrolls, is read. Ruth, a convert to Judaism, is welcomed when she returns to the Land of Israel with her mother-in-law, Naomi, after they become widows and lose their wealth. It is a story of love and acceptance, setting a path for her future descendant, King David.

Shavuot is one of the three major pilgrimage festivals, with the other two being Passover and Sukkot. Dairy food is eaten to symbolize how the Torah feeds the mind and milk nourishes the body. Synagogues and homes are decorated with flowers, greens, and fruits. This holiday is very child-friendly: As the Torah and Ten Commandments show how to live an honorable life, children can learn how to share and act with empathy and kindness.

Late Night at the Cousins Comedy Club
(Featuring the Playroom Players)

Penny said, "Since grown-ups are supposed to stay up all night on Shavuot to study the Torah, let's invite *everyone* for a sleepover!"

"Where am I supposed to put them all?" Emma shook her head.

"Don't worry," answered Beni. "Who's sleeping?!"

"The last time we did that was for Sukkot," added Penny.

"When all the cousins had a sleepover in Sophie's sukkah."

"You mean *tried* to sleep," Milo corrected her. "It poured."

Emma and Beni made a list: "There's Cousins Max and Rosie, and Max's partner, Avi; your sister, Sara, Harry, and Liam; Cousin Goldie, her husband, Abe, and Noa; Cousin Molly and Sophie; and Cousin Sam, his wife, Luna, and Baby Becky. And Aunt Izzy and Uncle Gus, if they're not too busy with their catering."

"You forgot Mama and Papa, and us!" shouted Milo and Penny.

On Shavuot, Beni and Emma threw an over-the-top party!

There were ice-cream cones and sodas and floats and sundaes.

There were several kinds of cheesecake, even though Emma was not a fan. She had a cherry-cheese Danish instead.

There were noodle puddings. Salads. Appetizers. Fruit. And lots of blintzes: cheese, apple, blueberry, and potato-mushroom.

The cousins ran around the house while their parents talked.

Great-grandma Mindel called them "*Vilde chayas*. Wild things!"

But that didn't stop them. It was like watching a roller coaster.

Near bedtime, Penny said, "Let's have an ice-cream joke contest!"

They made a large sign and put it in the hall near the playroom:

LATE NIGHT AT THE COUSINS COMEDY CLUB
Featuring "The Playroom Players"
Free Tonight Only, Downstairs at Beni's Place
(Black Box by the Basement Boiler)
One Drink Minimum: Ice-cream Soda or Float

"I'll start," said Liam. "Where do you learn about Shavuot?"

He answered his own joke without pausing, "In *sundae* school!"

"What happened when I thought I saw the ghost of Elijah?"

Milo jumped in as everyone shouted together, "What?"

"*I screamed*! Get it? *Ice cream!* It was really Papa at the door!"

"*Oy*, we got it!" they groaned. Then it was Sophie's turn.

"What did the news reporter say? I've got an inside *scoop*!"

Noa was up next. "How do you make an elephant float?"

"How?" Everybody rolled their eyes in anticipation.

"Take one elephant, add seltzer, syrup, and two scoops
of vanilla ice cream."

"That's a good one!" Milo giggled as Noa went offstage.

Penny ended with, "What do you get when you cross a yeti
with an ice-cream sandwich?" There was no reaction.

"Frostbite!" Penny hollered.

"I don't get it!" said Milo, while Liam added, "Neither do I."

"Get her off!" they shouted together.

And the parents yelled back, "No hecklers allowed!"

Baby Becky sat on Cousin Sam's lap, licking his ice-cream pop
like a pacifier. Rainbow sprinkles freckled her chubby cheeks.

Sam wrapped her in a blanket like a *blintze* after the show.

"Well, that was some performance!" praised the parents.

"A Purim spiel, a Passover sing-along, and now this!"

"We started celebrating the holidays in September.

Will we begin a new year at the end of this summer?

And get new calendars again?" the cousins wondered.

Beni said, "Why not? It can become our new tradition!"

The holidays are for sharing jokes, art, music, songs, dance, food, and laughter. And of course, telling tiny tales about everyone in the family.

Or as Great-grandma Mindel would say, "The whole family—*gantse mishpachah*."

And then they did an enormous group hug.

Cousins on the inside. Grown-ups on the outside.

In one never-ending and never-beginning circle of love.

Beni raised a glass as the others joined in: "To life! *L'chaim!*

Happy holidays around the year! *Chag Sameach!*"

BENI'S BLINTZES

On Shavuot, dairy is served. Beni learned how to make blintzes watching his great-grandma Mindel, when she came up from Miami Beach in the summer and stayed at their house. They would freeze the batch and defrost them right in time for Shavuot. She made classic plain cheese. But there are other fillings: cherry, blueberry, apple, and savory potato-mushroom.

BATTER

4 large eggs

1 cup milk

⅓ cup cold water

Pinch of salt (optional)

1 tablespoon sugar

½ teaspoon vanilla extract

1 cups unbleached all-purpose flour

FILLING

½–1 pound cottage cheese

8 ounces farmer cheese

2 tablespoons granulated sugar

¼ cup dark raisins (optional)

½ teaspoon ground cinnamon

1 stick butter or margarine (for frying)

1. Beat eggs, milk, water, salt, sugar, and vanilla in a large bowl.
2. Blend, adding flour. Mix until batter is smooth. Set aside.
3. In another bowl, combine filling ingredients. Refrigerate for 15 minutes.
4. Heat a 9-inch frying or omelet pan with curved sides. Grease with butter. Pour half-filled ladle in center of hot pan. Lift pan to rotate, coating bottom and forming a large thin crepe pancake (blintze).
5. Cook for 1 minute or less until it has light brown splotches and blisters. Fry only one side and flip crepe onto a plate. (Melt more butter every fourth crepe to prevent it from sticking to the pan while frying.)

6. *To make blintzes*: Spoon each pancake with 2 tablespoons of filling on cooked side of crepe in center. Roll up sides one on top of another like an envelope to create a small package—the blintze! Then fold each end inside to create a rectangular package about 2 ½ by 4 inches. Repeat.

7. If you freeze or refrigerate before frying, wrap each blintze in parchment paper so they don't stick together and store in container.

8. *To fry blintzes*: Use nonstick pan or one with greased butter or margarine. Cook until light golden brown on each side. Flatten slightly with a spatula after you flip crepe over to get that blintze effect.

9. Serve hot with a side of sour cream or yogurt and berries (optional). (You can keep all blintzes in the oven at 300 degrees Fahrenheit until ready to serve.)

Yield: Approximately 1 dozen blintzes

Note: If farmer cheese is not available, use the equivalent by substituting quantity in dry-style small-curd cottage cheese.

GUS'S ICE-CREAM SODA

Beni's good friend Gus has a bagel bakery in Brooklyn. His daughters run a catering company in New York City dating back to their father's roots. They serve old-fashioned root beer floats, black-and-white sodas (chocolate syrup/vanilla ice cream), and malteds! (Like a milkshake.) Gus's younger sister, Sadie, used to make them in the 1950s for his friends after a game of handball in the park. He misses his favorite Roumanian East Village haunt that served an "egg cream," which has no eggs. U-bet chocolate syrup, milk, and seltzer. Stir. That's it!

1. In a tall glass, pour 1–2 tablespoons of any flavored syrup.
2. Add ½ glass milk (about 4 ounces). Fill the rest of the glass with seltzer or club soda until it is ¾ full.
3. Add 1 scoop of ice cream. Stir gently with tall spoon.
4. You can put whipped cream on top, but Beni's family like it plain. Particularly Gus. Very old-school.

Beni & Sara, younger, and Mama, at Gus's kid sister Sadie's Sweet Shop

Glossary

Afikomen (A-fee-KO-mun) Middle matzoh of three, half of which is hidden and later eaten as "dessert" during the Passover Seder.

Babaganoush (Ba-ba-gan-NOOSH) Spread of pureed baked eggplant, tahini (sesame) paste, olive oil, garlic, and lemon. Middle Eastern dish.

Babka (BAB-ka) A yeast cake made with chocolate or cinnamon and raisins swirled in the dough.

Bialys (Bee-OLL-lees) Flat, indented breakfast rolls (looks like little wading pools) sprinkled with sautéed chopped onions.

Blintze (BLINTZ) Yiddish word meaning "pancake." Crepe-filled pancake. Since it contains dairy, it is often served on the holiday of Shavuot.

Chag Sameach (HAG Sa-MAY-ach) "Ach" like in Bach. Happy Holiday.

Challah (HA-la) (pronounced throughout with guttural *ch* like in Scottish *loch* or like Bach) An egg-enriched yeast bread served at a Shabbat meal. A round challah is eaten during the holiday of Rosh Hashanah.

Chametz (Huh-mets) Hebrew for leaven-fermented dough, and anything that is not Kosher for Passover (grain, bread, cereal, noodles . . .).

Chanukah (HA-noo-ka) (also can be spelled Hanukkah) Eight-day Festival of Lights celebrating the victory of the Maccabee warriors over Antiochus IV, who tried to make the Jews believe in many gods instead of One God.

Chuppa (HUP-a) A wedding canopy.

Dayenu (Die-YAY-noo) Hebrew for "It would have been enough."

Days of Awe The holidays of Rosh Hashanah and Yom Kippur.

Dreidel (DRAY-del) A four-sided *sevivon*—spinning top used in a game played during Chanukah.

Elijah Custom is to leave a cup of wine and a door open for the Prophet Elijah during the Passover Seder in hope that he will return to earth.

Erev (EH-rev) Hebrew for "evening." Also means: "The day before a holiday." (Like in erev Passover.)

Etrog (EH-trogue) Citron (lemon-like) fruit used symbolically in prayer during Sukkot.

Falafel (Fa-LA-fel) Ground seasoned chickpea balls deep-fried in oil.

Falouris (fa-LUR-is) Indian fried chickpea pancakes.

Ganse Mishpacha (GON-sa Mish-PAW-kheh) The whole family.

Gelt (GELT) Money. Chocolate coins wrapped in gold paper given as little gifts during Chanukah. Used in the game Spinning a Dreidel.

Grogger (GROG-ger) Yiddish word for a noisemaker that is used to blot out Haman's name during the reading of the Megillah on Purim.

Haggadah (Ha-GAH-da) Hebrew for "telling." A special book read during the Seder by all gathered around the table—taking turns—that narrates the Passover story of the enslaved Jews' exodus from Egypt to freedom.

Hamantaschen (HA-mun-tash-en) Triangle-shaped pastries filled with jams eaten during Purim in remembrance. Named after the wicked Haman, who tried to destroy the Jewish people.

Haroset (HA-ro-set) (Also can be spelled Charoset.) A sweet paste of chopped nuts, apples, and wine that symbolizes the mortar that the enslaved Israelites used to build the pyramids in Egypt. (Some use chopped dates.)

Horah (HOE-ra) A joyous circle folk dance.

Hummus (HUM-miss) Middle Eastern dip/spread of mashed chickpeas and tahini with spices.

Kasha Varnishkas (KA-sha VARN-ish-kas) Buckwheat grains, boiled and sautéed in oil with chopped onions, mixed with boiled bowtie-shaped noodles.

Kibitzer (KIB-its-er) A jokester. One who teases and gives unwanted advice, making comments on the sideline.

Kiddush (Ki-DOOSH) A ceremonial blessing before the meal for the Sabbath (Shabbat) and holidays said over a cup of wine.

Kneidlach (K'NEYD-loch) Matzoh balls for chicken soup.

Kol Nidre (COAL NE-Dra) Prayer sung in synagogue at the beginning of the service on the eve of Yom Kippur.

Kugel (KOO-gull) A noodle or potato pudding.

Kvelling (k-VELL-ing) Bursting with pride.

Lag B'Omer (Log B-omer) Holiday takes place on the thirty-third day of the Counting of the Omer, a forty-nine-day period between Passover and Shavuot. In Hebrew, during ancient times, *omer*—a sheaf of barley—was offered in temple worship on the second day of Passover.

Latkes (LOT-kahs) Potato pancakes eaten during Chanukah.

L'Chaim (l'HIGH-em) Hebrew for "to life."

L' Shanah Tovah (Le Shah-NA Toe-VA) Hebrew for "good year." Happy New Year greeting during the holiday of Rosh Hashanah.

Lulav (LOO-lav) Palm branch waved and shaken during the Sukkot holiday.

Maccabee (MAC-a-bee) Hebrew for "hammer." Jewish warriors who drove out Antiochus IV's army were called Maccabees. The story is told during Chanukah.

Maggid (ma-GID) With a soft "g." The telling of the Passover story.

Mandelbrot (MAHN-del-braht) A dry, oblong-sliced almond cookie.

Matzoh (MOT-za) Flat unleavened "bread" eaten during Passover.

Matzoh balls Round soup dumplings made from matzoh meal.

Megillah (ma-gill-A) Hebrew for "scroll." The Scroll of Esther is read during Purim. She saved the Jews from destruction at the hands of the evil Haman, revealing his plot to the king.

Menorah (Me-NO-rah) A nine-armed candelabra; or *channukiah* or *hannukiah*. Eight arms represent each night of the Chanukah holiday. The ninth is for the *shammash* that lights the other candles.

Midrash (MID-rosh) Ancient sermons, stories, parables, allegories, told from the biblical texts and scriptures.

Mitzvot (mits-VOTE) Good deeds.

Oy Veh (oy-VAY) Yiddish expression showing frustration, like "Woe is me!"

Pareve (Parve) In Kashrut, the dietary laws of Judaism. Food without milk or meat in any form.

Passover Eight-day holiday commemorating the enslaved Jews' exodus from Egypt to freedom.

Plotz (PLOTS) To faint and collapse from exhaustion.

Purim (POOR-rim) Holiday celebrating the defeat of Haman's plan to kill all the Jews of Persia.

Rabbi (Ra-BYE) Spiritual leader of a synagogue who is an ordained teacher of Jewish law.

Rosh Hashanah (Rosh Ha-shan-NA) Hebrew for "head of the year." The holiday marks the start of the Jewish calendar and the beginning of the Days of Awe. Rosh Hashanah and Yom Kippur are called the High Holy Days (Days of Awe).

Rugelach (RU-ga-loch) Small rolled pastries filled with raisins, ground nuts, cinnamon, sugar, and different kinds of jams or chocolate.

Schmaltz (SHMALTZ) Rendered chicken fat.

Seder (SAY-dar) Hebrew for "order." This special, very long meal occurs on the first two nights of Passover (Pesach), during which time the story of Passover is narrated from the Haggadah and various ritual foods are eaten.

Shabbat (Sha-BAHT) Jewish sabbath.

Shalach Manot (SHA-loch MA-note) Sweet gifts of food and fruit (a Purim basket) are given to friends and the poor during the Purim holiday.

Shammash (Sha-MASH) Hebrew for "servant." The ninth arm of the menorah that holds the shammash "helper" candle that lights all the other candles for each of the eight nights.

Shavuot (Sha-vu-OAT) Holiday that celebrates the giving of the Torah on Mount Sinai. During this harvest festival, the Book of Ruth is read.

Shemini Atzerat (Sha-ME-ni Ot-ZER-it) Last day of Sukkot holiday, when there is a prayer for rain.

Shofar (Show-FAR) Hollowed ram's horn blown during the Rosh Hashanah holiday in synagogue services to announce the new year. It is sounded one hundred times during a traditional service.

Shvach (SHVACH) Tired, weak, faint.

Simchat (Sim-KA) Joy. A festive occasion.

Simchat Torah (Sim-KA TOE-ra) means "Joy of the Torah." This holiday marks the completion of the Torah cycle reading.

Sufganiyot (Suff-gan-E-oat) Doughnuts, fried and eaten during Chanukah.

Sukkah (Soo-KA) A temporary hut, partially open to the sky, often covered with palm branches, is built during Sukkot to remind the Jews of how the Israelites lived in the wilderness for forty years. Many Jews eat, sleep, and spend time in their sukkah during the weeklong holiday.

Sukkot (Soo-COAT) Feast of the Tabernacles is an eight-day holiday commemorating the final gathering of the harvest; a thanksgiving.

Synagogue (SIN-a-gog) Jewish house of prayer. Also called a temple or a shul.

Tashlikh (Tash-LEEKTH) Hebrew word for "to cast." A ritual in which bread crumbs are tossed into a flowing body of water, symbolizing the casting away of sins to start a new year afresh during Rosh Hashanah.

Tisha B'Av (TISHA b'av) Holiday commemorates the destruction of the ancient Temples in Jerusalem.

The Ten Plagues: Blood, Frogs, Lice, Beasts, Cattle Disease, Boils, Hail, Locusts, Darkness, and Death of Firstborn were visited upon Egyptians. During the Passover Seder, the list is recited by everyone around the table together as each person dips their pinky into their glass of wine and then a tiny drop is symbolically dipped onto their plate as each plague is mentioned. (A separate small plate is often used for this.)

Torah (TOE-ra) The first five books of the Jewish Bible. The Torah is referred to as "the Tree of Life."

Tu B'Shevat (Too-beh-SHVAT) Holiday that celebrates the Jewish New Year of Trees.

Vilde chaya (VIL-da HI-yahs) Means "wild animal" or "beast" in Yiddish.

Yom Ha'Shoah (YOM HA show-a) Holocaust Remembrance Day.

Yom Ha'Atzma'ut (YOM ha atz-ma-UTE) Israeli Independence Day.

Zeppole (ZEP-oll-las) Deep-fried dough balls sprinkled with sugar.

ACKNOWLEDGMENTS

Thanks to Steven Zalben, my in-house yeshiva bucher for reviewing the Judaism and Hebrew, and the Little, Brown Books for Young Readers production team: Annie McDonnell, Leyla Erkan, Angelie Yap, Saho Fujii, and Virginia Lawther. And gratitude to Christy Ottaviano, my wonderfully sensitive editor, for allowing me to take this journey again (with all her tiny notes and gifts); to my longtime agent, Elizabeth Harding, for her "zen" attitude in a world that isn't; to Roberta Harris at @berta.bakes—my forever friend (it wouldn't be the holidays without you guys!); Rahel Musleah; all my pals in our pandemic "super club," who helped to get me through this; with gratitude for the generous blurbs given by Betsy Bird, Mollie Katzen, Ruth Reichl, Adeena Sussman, Jane Yolen, Lee Zalben, and The Jewish Book Council (Simona Zaretsky, Evie Sapphire-Bernstein, Michal Hoshander-Malen). And most of all to my very immediate family—the most important people in my world. Alexander, who started the Beni series with one simple question: Why are there no Chanukah decorations during the holidays in our town? I am indebted forever. Jonathan, who arranged, set the scores and lyrics, and once again, as always, comes through. I love you both. Their wives, Marni Zalben and Kate Feather, with love. Penny, Milo, and Liam—the sun, the moon, and the stars. My husband, for living my life with you.

INDEX